to Len - wit[h]
and h[op]
me[rr]y h[o]l[i]d[a]y -

ALSO BY WILL H. THEUS

Savannah Furniture, 1735–1925

How to Detect and Collect Antique Porcelain and Pottery

HOW TO DETECT
AND COLLECT
ANTIQUE FURNITURE

HOW TO DETECT AND COLLECT ANTIQUE FURNITURE

Will H. Theus

Alfred A. Knopf   New York   1978

THIS IS A BORZOI BOOK
PUBLISHED BY ALFRED A. KNOPF, INC.

Copyright © 1978 by Will H. Theus

Library of Congress Cataloging in Publication Data
Theus, Will H. [date]
How to detect and collect antique furniture.
Bibliography: p.
Includes index.
1. Furniture—Collectors and collecting.
2. Furniture—Expertising. I. Title.
NK2240.T45 1978 749 77-16281
ISBN 0-394-40098-4
ISBN 0-394-73492-0 pbk.

Manufactured in the United States of America

First Edition

To my children,
Will and Charlton

Contents

Illustrations

Color Plates

"Baltimore chair," American side chair

Split-banister back armchair

Chippendale-style slant-top desk

Empire-style pier table

Sheraton-style chest of drawers

Queen Anne–style lowboy

Empire-style sugar chest

Queen Anne–style card table

Hepplewhite-style demilune card table

Federal-style chair

(FOLLOWING P. 114)

Acknowledgments

Grateful acknowledgment is made to the following people who kindly permitted photographs to be taken of their furniture: Mr. and Mrs. J. Ferris Cann, Jr., Mr. and Mrs. Carl Clausen, Dr. and Mrs. Edward F. Downing, Mrs. Charles Ellis, Mr. and Mrs. W. Claggett Gilbert, Jr., Emory L. Jarrot, Mr. and Mrs. Remer Y. Lane, Juliette Gordon Low Girl Scout National Center, Mr. and Mrs. DeCourcy E. McIntosh, Carl Meadows, Inc., Antiques, Mr. and Mrs. A. Minis, Jr., Owens-Thomas House Museum, the late Mr. D. Wilkie Rabey and Mrs. Rabey, Albert H. Stoddard III, and Mr. and Mrs. J. Randall Winburn.

Special appreciation is extended to Hansell W. Ramsey for his guidance with the photographs; to Robert D. Reid, Harvey Smith, Carl D. Wheeler, and Kurt Naninga for technical assistance; to my typists, Viola F. Schwaab and Mrs. William F. Summerell; to my photographer, Richard Neville; and to my daughter, Mrs. George E. Quaile, who drew the illustrations.

W. H. T.
Isle of Hope,
Savannah, Georgia
July, 1977

HOW TO DETECT
AND COLLECT
ANTIQUE FURNITURE

Introduction

Two tables stand side by side. They are similar—the same size, round, mahogany, both pedestal tables with a tripod base. They appear at a first casual glance to be of the same quality and value. Now, before making a decision, is the time to take a second look—a discerning, probing look. A closer examination will reveal that the wood of one table is the wrong color, the weight is too light, the tool marks and joinings are false, and the pedestal and top are of different woods. This table is not genuine. It is wrong.

This second look must be accompanied with the necessary knowledge of what to look for to determine whether or not an article of so-called antique furniture is authentic, all original, and of good quality. Almost any piece scrutinized in an unbiased and unhurried way, with the proper information in mind, will disclose its secrets.

All antique furniture should be what it claims to be. It is usually safe to assume an antique is authentic when it is purchased from a reliable and knowledgeable dealer. Often, however, a piece is acquired from a house sale, from an individual who knows nothing about it, or from a second-hand shop. In this case—or in any case—the buyer should have the necessary know-how to check the article in detail and decide its quality for himself. It is human to desire to get what you are paying for and not just a reasonable facsimile or a copy, and in the end it is the buyer who must bear the responsibility of the purchase.

There are several excellent, scholarly, and informative books already available that tell how to discover fakes, or when an article of "antique" furniture has had alterations or additions. But, for the most part, these books describe furniture of museum quality and that which is of interest to expert discriminating collectors who are buying the cream of eighteenth- and nineteenth-century furniture, the very rare pieces, and are willing to pay the high prices—usually in the four, five, and even six figures—that they command. This is a minority group in the antique field.

Today, with the ever-growing and absorbing interest in antiques, there are an enormous number of new buyers and collectors who are in the market, although they cannot afford the ultimate. However, they want good pieces and are eager to learn how to discover them. They want to purchase antique furniture that will be an addition to their homes, give pleasure by a growing knowledge of what it is, and increase in value with time—not factory-made pieces or articles that have been altered to attract the unwary.

This is a primer designed to point out the pitfalls in acquiring antique furniture, so that acquisitions will not only enhance a home and be a lasting pleasure to own but, as taste changes, can be disposed of without loss of money—and even possibly at a gain.

The furniture found throughout the United States is predominantly English and American. The furniture of greater popularity and value is that made during the eighteenth and nineteenth centuries. This primer will therefore endeavor to instruct the newcomer to the field in how to take a second look at furniture made in the styles of those years—furniture that was made for the ordinary person and not for the very rich or for stately homes, but furniture available to the average buyer, furniture that can be found on the market today.

The year 1700 is a convenient date to commence this

book. It was just two years later, in 1702, that Queen Anne became Queen of England. At that time a marked change came into furniture design. Forms began to follow the human shape, and comfort became a concern. In America there is little surviving furniture prior to the first years of the eighteenth century, which period also marks the beginning of English influence on American furniture.

I

Notes for
the Novice Collector

The collecting of antiques has been going on since the earliest of times. The following quote is from a letter written in April, 1610:

The fact that the Duke, in furtherance of his own reputation, as well as his interest and amusement, has begun to establish an art collection, with antiquities, statues, pictures, and all kinds of rare objects, and now intends to increase it, this I consider to be most praiseworthy and excellent. It will bring him much knowledge and recreation, and furthermore, some pieces will bring double the price paid when one wishes to sell them.

The majority of people do not claim to be collectors, but they enjoy antiques in their homes and want to acquire good and useful pieces. The average antique buyer's primary concern is in furnishing his home; thus he should forgo the purchase of any piece that does not fit into his personal scheme. In general, an antique should be acquired to be enjoyed or utilized, but its value as a financial investment should also be considered. Antiques, when bought wisely, are tangible evidence of a good investment. Though some people may doubt this at present-day prices, it is constantly being demonstrated that a good antique continues to increase in value. Young buyers of today have one thing in their favor: they do not remember the days when a Queen Anne highboy could be bought for six or eight hundred dollars, or a fine Federal-period chest of drawers for fifty or a hundred. Amazingly, they pay what older collectors consider outrageously high sums, but to the beginner are just today's prices. What will the next twenty years hold for them? The public certainly reflects confidence that antiques will continue to be a good investment. In spite of the extremely high prices, English and American antique pieces continue to sell madly, as increasing sales at shows and shops confirm. To have antique furniture prove to be not only a joy but an investment, it should be acquired with discrimination, knowledge, intelligence, awareness—and, most important, common sense.

Many factors must be taken into consideration when buying antique furniture. First, realize that it takes time and patience to examine an article thoroughly. Also, be sure not to hold a preconceived opinion, since a biased mind warps judgment and makes it impossible to read correctly the evidence that the piece contains. A word of warning: be suspicious of a "bargain," a concept that has loaded quantities of junk on the unwary. Also beware of fads. Fads often become difficult to live with over a lifetime. Be familiar with styles that generations of use have proved worthwhile because of their satisfying and functional design.

It will help your self-confidence and your ability to judge whether or not an owner is being honest to become acquainted with the specialized terms describing the various styles, pieces, and parts of furniture, decorative methods, and so on. To assist in this, the meanings of the terms in this book and those most encountered elsewhere are given in the Glossary at the end of the text.

The question "What is an antique?" is a natural consideration. For many years most people agreed with the United States Customs ruling that for an item to be called antique and to enter the United States free of duty, it must have been made prior to 1830. This ruling was changed in 1967. Now an article is passed free of duty providing it is a hundred years old. This is, in most cases, accepted as a proper way to designate antiques of American origin as well as imports. But other things contribute to making an antique authentic. Its artistic merit and aesthetic appeal must be considered. A purely mechanical production or a strictly utilitarian object would not be considered antique no matter how old it might be. A true antique must be the handmade product of an individual craftsman or group of craftsmen, and must reflect, within the limits of the medium, the personality of the maker or makers. Most important, an antique cannot be an object that comes out of a machine and would continue to come out no matter who pulled the lever.

The term "antique furniture" is vastly misused at the present time. Factory-made golden-oak furniture produced during the first quarter of the twentieth century is frequently referred to as "antique," and sold in shops as such, which further adds to the misconception. Correctly it should be termed "secondhand furniture" and should be priced commensurate with other secondhand furniture. Pedestal dining tables, convex glass-sided china cabinets, and pseudo-Jacobean sideboards selling in the high hundreds, and washstands and old kitchen chairs going for a hundred or more, are all overpriced. One reason for the current popularity of this furniture is that it has become mysteriously identified by the young with their desire to return to the life of the pioneer days, as demonstrated by the many who are living in communal groups on farms, wearing blue jeans or long calico skirts, and collecting tinware and Mason jars.

There is one justification in buying this furniture (but only if it is priced reasonably), and that is accepting it for what it is. A young couple beginning to furnish their home on a low income may prefer to get this in place of new, cheap, and poorly constructed furniture from a store. Golden oak is usually strong and durable. It can be painted or decorated without destroying the value, as would be the case with good antiques. With development of taste, increased income, and the desire to buy better pieces, the couple can usually dispose of this secondhand furniture for what they invested in it.

II

Style and Period

The first thing to determine when examining an article of furniture is the style in which it is designed. A style is what was in vogue during a certain period. Period, in the sense used here, is a length of time within well-defined historical limits. Furniture styles in England were named for the current rulers until the middle of the eighteenth century—such as Queen Anne (1702–1714) and Early Georgian (1714–1760)—since it was the ruling classes who fixed the styles. With the publication of Thomas Chippendale's *Gentleman and Cabinet-Maker's Director* in 1754, the styles began to be named for the designer-publicists. Chippendale's *Director* was followed in 1788 by a book of designs by George Hepplewhite called *Cabinet-Maker and Upholsterer's Guide*, then by Thomas Sheraton's *Cabinet-Maker and Upholsterer's Drawing Book* in 1791. New design books of Sheraton's continued to be issued until 1812.

An article of furniture is of a certain style when most of its features represent what was popular during a set period. However, furniture can be and is made in the style of a period at any time after that style was fashionable. Naturally, a piece could not have been made before that style was introduced. When such terms as "in the Queen Anne style" or "in the Chippendale style" are used, this does not necessarily mean that the furniture so described was itself made at that time, but was made in the style popular during that period. When the term "of the period" is used, however, it means the furniture so described was made during that period, or within the next few years, while the style was still in fashion. Too much stress cannot be placed on this, since it governs price to a large extent. A Chippendale-style chair of good quality made circa 1765 (of the period) would be of several times more value than a chair of similar style made in the 1860s and 1870s called "Centennial," or "in the Chippendale style."

It is possible to ascertain when certain styles of furniture were in vogue through various sources, such as book illustrations, contemporary prints, legal documents, bills of sale, newspaper announcements, cabinetmakers' advertisements, and design books. Inventories are of special value in determining what furnishings were used during certain periods. As early as June, 1633, a bill was passed in Plymouth, Massachusetts, which in part ordered "that the wills and testaments of those that die be proved orderly before the Governor and Council within one month after the decease of the testator and that a *full inventory*, duly valued, be presented with the same."

The most unreliable source of information in dating an antique is family tradition unsupported by evidence. Often a story gets associated with the wrong piece, or in dating an article the life span of each owner is added up, with no consideration of the fact that many of those years were lived simultaneously. Grandmother, who lived to the ripe old age of a hundred and five, did not necessarily own the piece from birth. Fortunately, our enjoyment of a good antique does not depend upon knowing exactly when or by whom it was made. Identifying the style and judging the approximate date are generally sufficient for the amateur collector.

III

Queen Anne Style

Queen Anne ascended the throne of England in 1702. The early eighteenth century is called the "walnut era," and saw the arrival of a new concept of furniture design. In this the age of expanded prosperity following the Duke of Marlborough's victories, many great estates and manor houses were built, and the owners were anxious for fine furnishings and financially able to acquire them.

The bulk of the furniture that has come down to the present time is, no doubt, from the houses of the merchant classes, since the period was one of great commercial activity. Judging from the simple and charming examples of English walnut furniture surviving, the standard of comfort and good taste among the middle classes was high.

The Queen Anne style marked a definite trend away from the rectangular and usually heavy style of the seventeenth century toward curves and lightness. Furniture attained a new standard of human comfort by the introduction of a greater variety of forms. For the first time, chairs were designed to fit the figure and showed functional expression. The crest rail of the back was curved so as to fit the nape of the sitter's neck, and in such way support the enormous and heavy wigs worn by both ladies and gentlemen of fashion in that period. The armrests on the open-arm chairs did not extend to the edge of the seat but stopped several inches short to allow ample room for the prodigious hooped skirts and wide whalebone-stiffened coats.

Queen Anne–style furniture has certain clearly defined

QUEEN ANNE CHAIRS

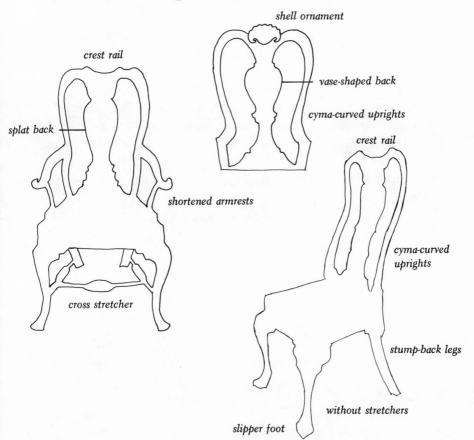

features of form that make it possible to distinguish it from antecedent types. The characteristics of the furniture are: simplicity; restrained ornament, beauty of form rather than decoration; and a silhouette of unadorned, controlled curves with little or no ornament. The C curve, S curve, and shell were the only forms of embellishment on carved pieces.

A departure in the design of furniture that had a far-reaching and lasting effect upon furniture styles—the. cabriole leg with shaped foot—was introduced in this period. The cabriole leg has been traced back to China and Egypt; it came to the Continent through Holland and France. It appeared on chairs, tables, sofas, and chests; in fact, on all forms of furniture raised from the floor. The name was adopted from the French word *cabriole*—a goat-leap—although it was not a literal description of the form. The early forms bore only a faint resemblance to the leaping leg of the animal; later forms were more realistic. Now the name is applied to almost any furniture leg built with a knee.

These early cabriole legs had stretchers. The stretchers were discarded when it was no longer necessary to protect the feet from the litter of a straw-strewn floor. The feet were either club, web, carved, pad and paw, or a very simple claw and ball. The knees were plain or carved, with a shell or two

CABRIOLE LEGS AND FEET

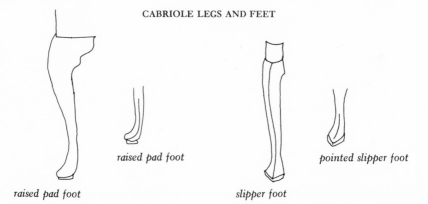

raised pad foot

raised pad foot

slipper foot

pointed slipper foot

small C curves on either side. The backs of the chairs had a tall vase or urn-shaped unpierced splat. By the Early Georgian era, decoration had become much more elaborate—more carving on the crest rail, pierced splats, heavily carved knees, and claw-and-ball feet. But Queen Anne proper was kept simple, and it was by shaping the lines into subtle curves, rather than by carving, that grace was imparted to the very form of the furniture. The serpentine or cyma curve, called by Hogarth "the line of Beauty," predominated. This is seen on the crest rails, uprights, legs, stretchers, arms of chairs, and the hooded tops and aprons of case pieces.

Every type of furniture was being made: chairs, tables, stools, mirrors, chests of drawers, tallboys, cabinets, secretaries, bureaus, writing tables, card tables, and clock cases. The colossal refectory and trestle tables of the previous era went out with the banquet hall; and small drop-leaf tables of various sizes made to seat from four to eight were being used, with several placed in a room so that the guests could gather in intimate groups.

Walnut, solid and veneered, was the wood generally used for Queen Anne furniture. Veneering consists of entirely covering one sort of wood with a thin layer of choice wood

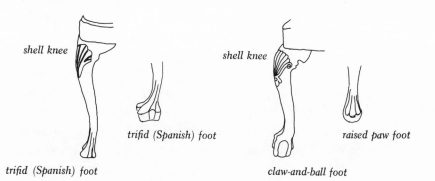

shell knee

trifid (Spanish) foot

trifid (Spanish) foot

shell knee

raised paw foot

claw-and-ball foot

such as burl walnut or mahogany. The object of veneering is not to deceive by giving the effect that the whole article is made of the finer sort of wood, but to make possible a greater choice of wood by applying these thin overlays, and to produce a more beautiful effect by combining the various grains. Veneering is often looked upon with disapproval, but the principle it stands for is perfectly straightforward. It would have been impossible to construct a great many cabinets of solid walnut, nor would the effect have been as pleasing. Expert workmanship was needed to make veneered furniture. Old veneers were cut by hand about an eighth of an inch thick. In the Queen Anne period, walnut veneering reached high perfection. Beautiful effects were produced by cross-banding various strips and diversifying the course of the grains and the shades. Oak was first used as a base; later on, commoner woods such as pine were used. A piece should not be considered inferior if the base is not of oak. In fact, oak was eventually discontinued, because the veneer had a tendency to pull away from it.

Marquetry, which is a combination of inlaying and veneering, was also a frequent feature of this period. It is produced by covering a surface with a veneer, cutting out the desired design, and filling it in with other woods.

Lacquered furniture "in the Oriental taste" was being fashioned in the last quarter of the seventeenth century and the first half of the eighteenth century. It reached the height of its popularity about 1710, but continued to be made for many years. Although it had been popular in Japan as early as the third century, it was not until late Tudor times that any specimens of Japanese or Chinese lacquer reached England, and then principally in the form of small cups, bowls, and trays. Lacquer was not imported to Europe on a large scale until just before 1600. The first English lacquer may have been produced soon afterward, but it did not become generally popular until the publication of the well-known *Treatise on Japanning and Varnishing*, by Stalker and Parker, in 1688. Quite a bit of English lacquered furniture survives. Various articles were lacquered, including secretary-bookcases, cabinets, long-case clocks, and chairs. Ground color was in several shades: black, tortoise-shell, green, and red—red being the most sought after.

Gesso was occasionally used on Queen Anne mirror frames. This is a process wherein a design is built into relief with layers of size and plaster, which are applied with a brush and usually gilded.

The fashions of furniture of the Queen Anne style lost their simplicity and, although holding to the same lines, became very ornate and rococo with the influence of the Hanoverian George I, who followed Queen Anne in 1714.

In America, by the end of the first quarter of the eighteenth century, there was no longer an entire log-cabin environment. Fine houses were being built in important cities —Boston, Salem, Newport, Philadelphia, New York, Charleston—along the Hudson River, and in Tidewater Virginia. The people who built the houses wanted to fill them with equally fine furniture, since one of the ways a family could display its wealth was through its possessions. By this time, encouraged by the current prosperity, many skilled craftsmen were plying their trade in these centers. There were not only cabinetmakers, but working in conjunction with them were carvers, gilders, turners, and chairmakers. In Boston there were a hundred and fifty of these craftsmen practicing their trade prior to the Revolution. Few of them can be identified, but the name of John Pimm is recorded on a label found on a handsome japanned highboy in the Queen Anne style. A japanner, Thomas Johnson, worked in Boston from 1732 to 1767, and it has been considered that he japanned the Pimm highboy. Names of craftsmen working in the early years of the eighteenth century are known through advertisements in local publications. The *South Carolina Gazette* of August 12, 1732, carried the following notice:

Broomhead & Blythe.—At New Market Plantation, about a mile from Charleston, will continue to be sold all sorts of Cabinet Work, chest of Drawers, and Mahogany Tables and Chairs made after the best manner; as also sorts of peer Glasses, Sconces, and dressing Glasses. Where all sorts of bespoke work is made at the lowest price, by Messrs. Broomhead & Blythe.

Thomas Elfe, of Charleston, first advertised in the *South Carolina Gazette* on September 28, 1747. From an extant account book, information can be gleaned of the quantities of furniture he made and for whom he made it. Cabinet-makers from other cities advertised as well.

The furniture made in settled America during the period took two forms. Simple, functional articles were usually made by local carpenters in the styles of the previous century, styles familiar to them from furniture they grew up with in their former countries. Pieces of this sort were constructed of local woods in patterns congenial with the needs of simple households. The alternative was furniture designed and made for fine houses by skilled craftsmen, who received their inspiration from architectural and furniture design books published by Englishmen such as John Vardy and William Jones, and by men who had learned their trade in their mother country. These designs in the Queen Anne and George I style were modified to reflect the originality of the makers and the requirements of their patrons. Virginia walnut was used for the most part, but also native woods: maple, the fruitwoods (cherry, apple, pear), butternut, ash, local oak, pine, and other easily available woods. The characteristics of the Queen Anne style—the simple C curves, the cabriole legs in

*Queen Anne–style small table, American, made in the South
circa 1740. Virginia walnut, cyma-curve-shaped top,
restrained cabriole legs terminating in raised trifid feet.*

varying forms, and the tall vase-shaped splat on chair backs
—were popular in America and, owing to the time lag, remained fashionable in some sections until the third quarter
of the eighteenth century (see color section, following p. 114).

These characteristics are typical of most of the furniture
of the early settlements in America, with the exception of
New York. The first New York furniture shows the influence
of the robust Dutch patroons in its generous proportions.
Reminiscent of the styles of Holland, the great chests are
simple and commodious, the chairs are wide-seated and
deep, and the tables simple and strong. In the Queen Anne
period that followed, the first distinctive New York characteristics are to be found. The shod pad foot was regional in
character, and the chairs showed a broad, sharply curved
splat.

Fashion has a strong, controlling influence over furniture
as it has over so many matters of taste. Certain articles of
furniture that originated in England lost favor there, but
continued to be made in America for many years. The gate-
leg table, usually constructed of oak, appeared in England at
the beginning of the seventeenth century, but after walnut
tables with cabriole legs came into vogue in England, out
went the previously popular gate-leg, except in provincial
areas.

The gate-leg table, whose legs were vase-and-ring turned
or baluster-and-ring turned, terminating in small knob, pear-
shape, or—occasionally—Spanish feet, was named for the
gate-like form of the swinging legs that support the drop
leaves. Constructed of walnut, straight-grained or curly
maple, and sometimes cherry or other native hardwoods,
they continued to be made in all sections of America until
the middle of the eighteenth century. The early ones are
scarce and priced high, but they have been reproduced in
large numbers in mahogany and other woods. Gate-legs en-

GATE-LEG TABLE

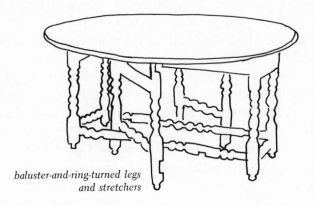

*baluster-and-ring-turned legs
and stretchers*

joyed a renewed popularity around the turn of the twentieth century and many copies were factory-made in mahogany and cherry. This is good reason to approach with caution the purchase of any gate-leg table claimed to be eighteenth century.

Simultaneous with the vogue of the gate-leg table was a chair of English parentage in the Carolean and William and Mary style called the "cane chair." It has a tall back with caned panel and seat, side uprights, and is joined with crests of carved Flemish scrolls. Some cane chairs have cross stretchers with the same scrolls, while others have turned legs terminating in a Spanish foot and boldly turned stretchers. So few of these were made in America that they may almost be dismissed. A more familiar example from the William and Mary period is the banister-back chair. (See color section following page 114.) Banister is a corruption of "baluster," the architectural term for the turned spindles supporting the handrail on the outer side of a stairway. The chair takes its name from the resemblance of the vertical splats that form the back to split banisters, since they are flat on the front and half round on the back. This treatment of the back was occasionally employed in provincial English pieces, but it is primarily an American achievement. From a carved and crested or shaped upper crosspiece to a simple one a little above the seat, four or five vertical splats provided the back. The shaping of the half-round splats varied, but essentially all were vase-and-ball turnings. The chairs were made with or without arms. The rear uprights were usually square from the seat level down, and above were turned in vase, ring, and ball designs except for short distances where the upper and lower crosspieces of the back were mortised into them. The front uprights were turned in like manner but, unlike the rear ones, were provided with feet—simple button, turnip, or the carved Spanish type, sometimes carried over to the Queen Anne cabriole leg to replace the simpler duck foot. The seats were always of twisted rush, and the upper crosspiece of the back, if not carved, had the effect of scroll-saw cutting. Maple was the most popular wood, although other hardwoods with a straight grain were used. However, the finish of the banister-back was universally painted: dark red, bottle-green, and black were the popular colors. These chairs were made in quantity in all the colonies as far south as Pennsylvania, and possibly Maryland and Virginia. Their heyday was from 1700 to about 1730, but simpler ones were produced in remote hill towns of New England much later.

A variation of these was a chair that, with the fiddle-back and cabriole leg, foretold the coming Queen Anne chair. The split-banister uprights were displaced by a single central splat in the shape of a fiddle; hence the chair was called fiddle-back. Actually, this is a misnomer, since the shaping of the back was inspired by the oviform vases imported from China, which were at the time in great favor. Except for the back piece, the chairs adhered in construction to that of the banister-backs, and were made in two types. The more elaborate had turned-and-square front legs terminating with

English Windsor armchair, circa 1735.
Yew with elm saddle seat.
Cyma-shaped center splat between spindles.
Sturdy cabriole legs pointed by H-shaped stretchers.

Flemish feet, boldly turned front and side stretchers, and back uprights more or less square and shaped to conform to the body by a slight backward curve above the seat level. These models, like the banister-backs, were made with or without arms; the seats were rush or, in the simpler ones, woven splint. The design originated about 1715, but was not adopted by working craftsmen except in the part of New England bordering on Long Island Sound or the Atlantic on the east. It was the forerunner of the Queen Anne chair, with cabriole front legs, vase-shaped splat, and tall conforming back surmounted by a carved yoke-shaped crest.

The first English Windsor chairs date from the end of the seventeenth century, and they continued to be made during the next two centuries. The Windsor chair "emigrated" to America from England during the first years of the eighteenth century, but there is a vast difference in Windsor chairs made in England and those made in America. The English version nearly always had arms. The best were of yew, the seat usually of elm. The legs of the English Windsor are not widely splayed and often not stretcher-based. Some have front cabriole legs terminating in Dutch feet. Frequently there is a shaped and pierced splat in place of the central spindle. The woods favored by the American Windsor chair-makers were pine for the saddle seats; maple, birch, ash, or chestnut for the turned legs. Spindles were steamed and made of ash, hickory, and oak. These chairs, unlike the English ones, were usually painted, green being the most popular color, but red, yellow, or black was also used. They are now catalogued according to the style of the back: comb back, bow back (or hoop back), fanback, low back, and the New England armchair, with continuous arm and back. With the addition of a shelf, the chair is called a writing-arm Windsor. They were made until about 1850.

Another article of furniture that is more American than

American Windsor chairs, circa 1800.
Hickory, pine, and maple saddle seats;
bamboo turned spindles and splay legs joined by stretchers.

English is the table-chair or hutch table. It serves as a chair when the top is raised and as a table when lowered. Many have box seats with lids that open to act as chests for storage. These were made in England as early as the late sixteenth century but were not produced in any great quantity after that. In America they were made chiefly in New England, with a pine top and often a base of oak.

The butterfly table is strictly an American development, possibly inspired by the English gate-leg table. A butterfly

Queen Anne–style highboy, American, made in New England circa 1750. Cherry, cyma-shaped apron, cabriole legs with raised slipper feet.

table is a drop-leaf table in which the leaves are supported by wing brackets and not by gate legs. The name came from the resemblance of the brackets or supports to the wings of the butterfly. It has a round, oval, or rectangular top with square or rounded edge. The four splay or rake legs are baluster or vase-and-ring turned, terminating in knob feet. They were made only in Connecticut, southern Massachusetts, and possibly Rhode Island, of plain or curly maple, walnut, or cherry, from 1700 to about 1750. They are very rare and in great demand.

The highboy, termed "tallboy" in England, is another article of furniture that was made in America long after it had gone out of fashion in England. First made in England at the beginning of the Restoration period, circa 1660, it went out of style around 1714, the beginning of the Georgian period. In America, on the contrary, the highboy continued to be popular until about 1770.

The furniture made in America prior to the Revolution is called Colonial. This term can be applied only to furniture made while America was a British colony, and should not be used in describing primitive or country furniture after 1776, when America was no longer a colony. It is also referred to as Early American furniture.

BUTTERFLY TABLES

IV

The Chippendale
Style

The style of furniture current during the third quarter of the eighteenth century is classified as Chippendale. For the first time, a style bears the name of a private individual, a designer-craftsman. This change resulted from the fact that Thomas Chippendale (c. 1718–1779) chose to publicize himself in the grand manner by bringing out a book illustrating his furniture designs. Known ever afterward as simply the *Director*, it was published in 1754 under the title

The Gentleman and Cabinet-Maker's Director. Being a Large Collection of the most elegant and useful designs of household Furniture in the Gothic, Chinese and modern taste: including a great variety of book-cases for libraries or private rooms, commodes, library and writing tables, china-cases, hanging shelves, tea-chests, trays, fire-screens, chairs, settees, sophas, beds, presses and clothes-chests, pier-glass sconces, slab frames, brackets, candle-stands, clock-cases, frets, and other ornaments. The whole comprehended in one hundred and sixty copper plates neatly engraved, calculated to improve and refine the present taste, and suited to the fancy and circumstances of persons in all degrees of life.

> *Dulcique animos novitate tenebo.* Ovid
> *Ludentis speciem dabit et torquebitur.* Hor.

By Thomas Chippendale of St. Martin's Lane, Cabinet-maker, London, Printed for the author and sold at his house in St. Martin's Lane. MDCCLIV. Also by T. Osborne, Bookseller in Gray's Inn; H. Piers, Bookseller, in Holborn; R. Sayer, Print-seller in Fleet Street; J. Swan, near Northumberland-House, in the Strand; At Edinburgh by Messrs. Hamilton and Balfour; and at Dublin by Mr. John Smith, on the Blind-Quay.

A second edition was published in 1755 with a few minor corrections. In 1762 a third edition was published, retaining ninety-five of the hundred and sixty plates of the first edition and adding a hundred and five new ones, for a total of two hundred plates. This *Director* made available to anyone who wanted to buy it a broad sampling of the furniture being made at the middle of the eighteenth century for the great English estates, as well as for the many simpler manor houses. What a wide category of furniture it covered! Whatever the demanding eighteenth-century English gentleman—constantly vying with his neighbor to create the finest furnished dwelling in his new golden age of leisure, taste, intellectual curiosity, and culture—desired, either for beauty or for function, was designed and executed merely on his whim. In contrast, the craftsmen who produced these much-perfected pieces had spent seven long years of apprenticeship and training and worked twelve to fourteen hours a day to maintain their strict standards.

Craftsmen figured prominently among the subscribers to

the first edition of the *Director*. It was for their benefit that
the proportions of pieces were stressed and that careful and
detailed measurements were given. Nevertheless, furniture
executed from the designs of Chippendale and other makers
(and this occurred most frequently in the provinces and the
American colonies) was generally altered and simplified,
and the end product bore only a superficial resemblance to
the published plate, although it retained the good line and
proportion of the original.

Chippendale, a name handed down through successive
generations, has come to signify quality and elegance. Although there are no label pieces of Chippendale furniture, it
is known through bills of sale that he provided furniture for
many fine houses. Because his bills were preserved, more of
Chippendale's furniture than that of any other maker has
been identified. However, there were at least half a dozen
other excellent cabinetmakers working in London during
and following the mid-eighteenth century, as well as many
lesser men who were practicing the trade. Chippendale himself employed about forty-five journeymen, who in turn set
up their own shops in England and America. Some of these
contemporaries actually surpassed Chippendale in cabinetwork and carving. Among them were William Vile, John
Cobb, Pierre Langlois, John Channon, and William Hallett.
But Chippendale, by publishing his book, gave his name to a
style that was adopted throughout most of England and imitated in varying degrees all over Europe and America. This
primer makes no attempt to attribute characteristics of workmanship or design to any particular cabinetmaker. The practice of assigning furniture to a certain maker on inadequate
evidence is increasing, and the results are questionable and
should be accepted with great caution. However, knowledge
of certain features will aid in identifying furniture that was
produced during the mid-eighteenth century in England and

somewhat later in America as being "in the Chippendale style."

Mahogany began to supersede walnut in English furniture during the second quarter of the eighteenth century, but by 1750, the beginning of the Chippendale period, it rapidly took over almost completely. It was tougher, stronger, and more elastic than any material heretofore used. Mahogany could be treated by methods, previously impossible, that resulted in superior elegance of line and lighter form. Elements of flexibility that are visible in the carcasses of some of the cabinetwork are the serpentine front, the small interior drawers with concurrent curves in reduced scale, and the sweeping and free bombé fronts and sides of case pieces. Nearly all Chippendale-style furniture in mahogany was without any inlay, and used carving for ornamentation with mounts of brass and sometimes of silver and copper.

Of all pieces of furniture, chairs are the most sensitive to new influences and the quickest to indicate a change of style. Chippendale, in his 1754 edition of the *Director*, gave fourteen plates to chairs, illustrating thirty-eight new designs. The most extensive section illustrated twelve "new-pattern

CHIPPENDALE CHAIR

pierced splat back

chamfered legs

H-shaped stretcher

pierced splat

pierced ladderback

chairs" of the type generally associated with his name. These are usually in mahogany and in a variety of patterns and ornamentation, in the rococo taste, frequently showing a modified cabriole leg with a carved leaf ornament on the knee, terminating in a scroll or curl-over foot. The already developed claw-and-ball foot was typical of the period. The straight, square, chamfered leg came into fashion about 1750, the cabriole leg having been in almost exclusive use for nearly fifty years. Often these straight legs were joined by stretchers. In some cases the legs and stretchers were quite plain, but this form also lent itself to perforation and an enrichment of applied frets and fret cornices. The general outline of the Early Georgian chair backs continued, with the center splat pierced, perforated, interlaced, and fret-patterned. Chippendale continued to employ in his designs the elaborate C and S scrolls. A central openwork splat was surmounted by a toprail of undulating serpentine or cupid's-bow form. Great strength was a feature of his chairs, since he took pains to make them durable by fixing the chair splat

CHIPPENDALE LEGS AND FEET

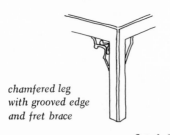

*chamfered leg
with grooved edge
and fret brace*

*fluted chamfered leg
with fret brace*

*acanthus-carved cabriole leg
with claw-and-ball foot*

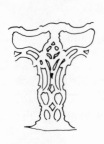

Strap-pierced back

Gothic-pillar or tracery back

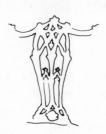

Chinese-influenced fret back

into the frame of the back, a practice not always followed by subsequent makers.

The back is the most distinctive feature of a chair and supplies the key for the proper classification. With this in mind, the illustrations above can be useful in identifying Chippendale chairs:

1. *Splat backs.* They were either flat or beaded and carved, vertically pierced, or pierced in various patterns in which C scrolls, singly or in combination, and Gothic features were frequently fashioned.

2. *Square or flat hoop backs.* These were found in the chairs of the Early Georgian period prior to the *Director* style, and presented a transition from the Queen Anne–Early Georgian hoop back to the later back with cupid's-bow toprail. They were rarely made after the mid-eighteenth century.

3. *Ribbon backs.* These chair backs were intricately designed and elaborately carved, usually introducing cords, tassels, and flowers, as well as interlaced and knotted ribbons. These were distinctly English of Chippendale's early period and not found in chairs made by American cabinetmakers.

4. *Gothic-pillar, bar, or tracery backs.* In these, the back was divided by slender clustered pillars supporting the arches of the toprail or was filled with molded or fretted Gothic traceries.

5. *Fret backs.* These were often filled with fretwork of Gothic influence or the conglomerate characters of Chinese designs.

Simple geometrical repeats without any specific influence were also made.

6. *Ladderbacks.* These had horizontal bars or slats between the two uprights, and continued the pattern of the toprail. They were flat, molded, or carved, and usually pierced or often interlaced.

7. *Square backs.* These were on upholstered-back chairs, both arm and side. The framework was at times fretted on Chinese patterned chairs.

On all the chairs the uprights were flat, molded, fluted, carved, or embellished with applied frets, according to the style and degree of elaboration.

The title page of the *Director* listed every type of furniture that was illustrated. It is a curious fact that the dining table was disregarded by compilers of trade catalogues during this period. It was not illustrated in the first edition of the *Director*, although there were six designs for open pedestal library tables and designs for French commode tables, as well as for writing, breakfast, and china tables. The dining table of the

CHIPPENDALE LOW CHESTS OF DRAWERS

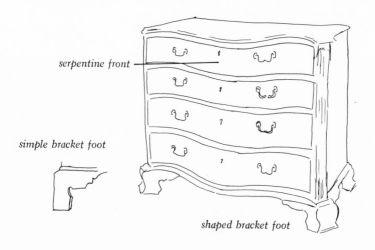

serpentine front

simple bracket foot

shaped bracket foot

time was usually composed of two, three, or more separate tables or parts, which were constructed so as to fit together as needed, forming one extended table. It appeared as a plain, functional article, allowing small range for the talents of the designer. If it took the form of a pair of tables, each was normally provided with one drop flap and was supported on five legs, one leg being hinged to the frame and swinging out on the inner side so as to support the flap when raised. The dining table was also frequently composed of three units, a center with rectangular extension flaps and a pair of semicircular ends. The ends were detachable and could be used independently as wall or side tables. This type of dining table persisted throughout the whole of the latter half of the eighteenth century.

Chests of drawers were of two varieties, low and high. The low ones were supported on short cabriole legs with claw-and-ball feet or on shaped bracket feet. There were ordinarily four drawers. The fronts of the drawers either over-lapped the rails slightly and were edged with a small convex molding called "lipped edge" or else were cock-beaded. The

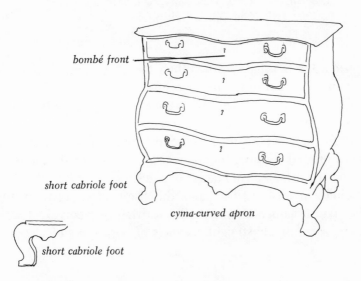

bombé front

short cabriole foot

cyma-curved apron

short cabriole foot

*Chippendale-style side table with drawers,
English, circa 1770. Mahogany, cock-beaded drawers
with bail handles, chamfered legs.*

lipped edge is usually earlier than the cock-beaded, which remained in use throughout the century.

The fronts were straight or shaped in either serpentine or bombé form.

High chests were similar to the low chests, with four additional drawers forming the top section. These double chests, or chests on chests, had bracket or swelled bracket feet with a carefully molded cornice, and the frieze often contained elaborate ornamentation of either carving or fretwork. The fronts were usually straight. Corners of both types of chests occasionally contained quarter-round fluted pilasters terminating in a capital at the frieze.

Sideboards with drawers and cupboards were not among the furniture of this period. Instead there were elaborate, rectangular, oblong sideboard tables, supported on four and sometimes six legs, more often square, straight chamfered than cabriole in form. These tables could have a single long frieze drawer. The tops were either of wood or of marble.

In this age of elegant living, homes were embellished with every type of furniture, much of the decoration showing foreign influence. The shells of the French rococo were an inspiration, as well as Chinese pagoda motifs and Gothic pointed arches and quatrefoils. An inventory of a stately mansion of this time would include chairs, stools, settees, sofas, day beds, bedsteads, tables, chests, chests of drawers, chests on chests, highboys, cabinets, secretaries, desks (see color section, following p. 114), writing tables, bookcases, cupboards, dining tables, sideboard tables, wardrobes, clothespresses, console cabinets or commodes, pedestals, guéridons, candlestands, wine coolers, fire screens, hanging shelves, elaborate mirrors, and tall clocks. Gilded sconces and girandoles illuminated the rooms.

In America from about 1760, cabinetmakers were using a free interpretation of the engraved plates from Chippendale's *Director*, producing an inexhaustible variety of furniture forms to which the name of Chippendale is now given. Commercial prosperity at the middle of the eighteenth century further stimulated the demand for grand houses and furnishings. Many cabinetmakers, carvers, and gilders, fortified with their London training as a recommendation for their services, emigrated to America. These craftsmen, to their surprise, found as competitors numerous native-born cabinetmakers who were not a bit reticent about their ability to

Chippendale-style Pembroke table, American,
made in New England circa 1770.
Cherry, fluted, chamfered legs joined by
exceptionally fine pierced cross stretchers.

improve on imported wares. There was a well-established
Colonial interest in the newest fashions in European decorative arts, spurred on by frequent travels, commerce, and
correspondence. Notwithstanding, the colonists were not
completely dependent on English models for their furniture.
The work of the local cabinetmakers was executed with free-
dom and imagination and frequently departed widely from

standard designs. Individuality was evident in American furniture. The colonists were English, Scots, Welsh, Irish, Hollanders, and French Huguenots. A few Germans, Swiss, Swedes, and Spanish and Portuguese Jews added even more diversity. The craftsmen remembered the furniture they had left behind in the mother country and used those prototypes as models. Local schools of furniture-making evolved certain distinctive characteristics, not only dependent on the craftsmen's country of origin but also on their religious beliefs. This is especially evident in crafts made by the Moravians and the Shakers, where functional furniture was well constructed in a simple, honest fashion by men who were expressing a tenet of deep religious belief. The Moravians first landed in Georgia in 1736; they came by way of England, having earlier been driven out of their native Bohemia and Moravia by religious persecution. Owing to various trials, early attempts to settle in Georgia were soon abandoned and many left to colonize in Pennsylvania, where Bethlehem became their central town. When, in 1752, Lord Granville sold the Moravians a 98,985-acre tract in North Carolina, a handful of pioneers made the arduous journey south from Pennsylvania and settled the town that was later to become

SHAKER CHAIR

Salem, North Carolina. The German Moravian influence can be seen especially in Pennsylvania and in the Piedmont sections of North Carolina and Georgia. It was not until late in the eighteenth century and into the mid-nineteenth century that the Shakers, who emigrated from England in 1774, had any significant colonies.

Chippendale-style side chairs, American,
circa 1770. Mahogany.
LEFT: *Pierced diamond-shaped splat, serpentine crest rail*
centered with shell carving, slip seat, cabriole
front legs, shell-carved knees, claw-and-ball feet.
RIGHT: *Pierced ladderback,*
serpentine crest rail, slip seat,
groove-edged, chamfered legs joined by stretchers.

For the most part, the same types of furniture produced in England were being made in America, showing related points of the Chippendale style. In the colonies, as in England, acanthus leaves, cockleshells, reverse scrolls, fluted columns, carved flower-and-ribbon moldings, bands of pierced frets, and gadrooned borders were the usual decorations employed in a vast array of combinations. Both cabriole and straight, square chamfered legs were characteristic of American Chippendale furniture. The cabriole leg terminated in the claw-and-ball foot, the paw foot, or the more urbane scrolled foot.

In two areas especially, Rhode Island and Philadelphia, there arose master craftsmen whose identity and identified pieces are now well established. At Newport there was the Townsend-Goddard dynasty, made up of Job and Christopher Townsend (1700–1765); John Goddard, son-in-law of Job (1724–1785); and John Townsend, son of Christopher (1732–1809). These men brought the block-front and shell style to its full development. This was an Americanized version of English design.

In Philadelphia gifted disciples of Chippendale included William Savery (1721–1787); Jonathan Gostelowe (1744–1795); and Benjamin Randolph (1762–1792). It was in Philadelphia that the design of the highboy and lowboy was refined and elaborated to a sophisticated artistic triumph. As mentioned in the preceding chapter, the highboy had lost favor even in provincial areas in England by the middle of the eighteenth century, but American craftsmen continued making it until the latter part of the eighteenth century. Highboys were executed in mahogany, and the cabriole leg with ball foot replaced the simpler Queen Anne pad foot. The glory of these Philadelphia pieces was in the carving. The ball-and-claw feet were boldly done, and decorated at the knees with acanthus-leaf carving. The front corners of both highboys and lowboys were either chamfered and fluted or had inset quarter-round fluted pilasters. The skirt was deeply valanced, and generally at the center there was a shell carved in relief that might be flanked by shallow leaf-carving. The front of the center drawer of the lower tier was always decorated with a shell-carved intaglio in a circle. High-fashion Chippendale-style furniture was also being produced in other sections of America.

ABOVE: *Chippendale-style block-front kneehole desk
with carved shells, American, made in Newport, R. I.,
1760 to 1775, probably by Edmund Townsend. Mahogany.
Top drawer has a center concave shell
with convex shells on either side,
original brass batwing plates with bail handles,
swelled bracket feet.*
OPPOSITE PAGE: *Chippendale-style corner cupboard, American,
made in the South, circa 1765.
Hard southern pine, shaped cornice with dentil molding,
paneled chamfered corners.*

It must be taken into consideration that while there were established rich families who wished to furnish their homes in the most up-to-date manner, they were a minority. There were a large number of colonists who were building comfortable homes and furnishing them with simple, functional furniture. They engaged their local cabinetmakers to fill their orders for furniture of good design, without embellishments and sturdy enough that it has withstood the usage of two hundred years. Furniture of this class is what the young collector is looking for to furnish his home. Refined, ornate furniture made by the skilled urban craftsman is now in a price range to attract only museums or the very discriminating collector with unlimited funds. Simple, well-made furniture in the Chippendale style was made throughout settled America during the latter years of the eighteenth century. Mahogany was the wood most used, but this furniture was also constructed in walnut, maple, fruitwoods, pine, and occasionally magnolia, butternut, and other woods indigenous to certain locations. This furniture fits into contemporary homes as well as restored houses.

V

The Neo-Classical Revival

Circa 1760-1800

The style and feeling of the last quarter of the eighteenth century were in distinct contrast to the dominant rococo, Chinese, Gothic, and French trends of the previous years. Soon after 1760, when George III ascended the throne, a new simplicity and severity of form in furniture structure appeared. This reversal of taste arose from the interest in classic remains that had been inspired by the recent excavations at Herculaneum and Pompeii. The main interpreters of the neo-classical movement in England were the Adam brothers, James and Robert.

Robert Adam, who had studied in Italy from 1754 to 1758 and was the leader of the movement, had settled as a practicing architect in England by January of 1758. *Ruins of the Palace of the Emperor Diocletian at Spalatro in Dalmatia,* by Robert Adam, F.R.S., F.S.A., Architect to the King and to the Queen, was published in 1764. This book was the first publication of Britain's then current most popular architect, although he had been practicing for several years and had gained an immense patronage. Patrons and critics alike eagerly accepted this lavish production, which was in keeping with the contemporary practice of self-advertisement. It had become a status symbol to have the Adam brothers "redo" your house. Stately mansions that had been completed only a few years previously underwent the alteration from Palladian, baroque, or rococo to the newly popular classic style, and with the change the house was fitted with furniture made from Adam designs. Though Adam was primarily an architect, his desire for complete harmony in the interiors of his buildings necessitated supervision of all details of household equipment. The interior architecture of his houses—the walls, furniture, and fittings—followed a single theme, consistently applied. Similar patterns and ornaments were employed in ceilings and carpets, overmantels and overdoors. Curtain boxes, pier glasses, girandoles, commodes, tables, picture frames, even the handles and lock plates of doors and furniture, were designed to be the harmonious parts of one scheme. It was truthfully said that when Adam designed a house he designed everything, from façade to fire irons. Sketches for ceilings, friezes, doors, grates, chimney pieces, mirrors, side tables, silver plate, locks, and a sedan chair were included in the plans submitted to a client. He deemed no detail too trivial or unimportant to receive his personal attention.

Adam's revolution in furniture design began in the late 1750s and early 1760s when the heavy George II furniture of French, Gothic, and Chinese rococo designs (which Chippendale had so recently imitated and popularized) was still in vogue. Remember it was only in 1754 that the first edition of the *Director* was published. Robert Adam almost single-handedly turned the tide in favor of classical design.

The contour of the furniture achieved by Adam struck a new note. The curving structural lines popular during the Chippendale period gave way to a rectilinear—or, rather, an angular—element. Although curving lines were used occasionally on serpentine fronts, demilune tables, and console cabinets, the directness of the straight structural line asserted itself. The furniture was lighter and more graceful in character. Legs were frequently tapered and had spade feet; other legs were rounded and usually fluted.

The various forms of decorative design used by Adam may be classed as architectural, floral, and animal. The architectural features were swags, both floral and drapery; beading; guilloche interlacings; paterae, both circular and oval; masques; Ionic capitals; anthemion or classic honeysuckle; urns; vases; minute and varied Pompeian details; spandrel fans; and egg-and-dart moldings. Floral motifs include pendant husks, water leaves or endives, roses, palmettes, pineapples, acanthus leaves, and fuchsia. The animal motifs were rams' heads, goats' heads, lions' heads, griffins, birds, and human figures.

ADAM DETAILS

birds and acanthus leaves
architectural detail

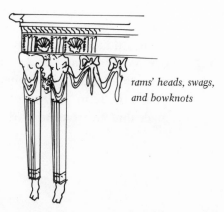

rams' heads, swags,
and bowknots

Much of the furniture was executed in mahogany, which remained strongly entrenched in popular favor, but the Adam brothers used many of the lighter woods, such as satinwood, Amboyna, harewood (sycamore stained), and various other woods seldom before seen except in inlay or marquetry. Painting and gilding were extensively employed. Combined with the delicate floral wreaths, ribbons, and minute Pompeian motifs were small panels, plaques, or cartoons painted by such well-known artists as Angelica Kauffmann and Giovanni Battista Cipriani. Satinwood furniture was only partially painted, since the color made a desirable background. Articles intended to be wholly covered with paint or gilding were constructed of pine or beech.

Holly and ebony and other precious woods were used for inlay. On exceptional pieces, Wedgwood plaques of jasperware were applied. Marble was used extensively for cabinet tops. Composition or compo of whiting, resin, and size, made from Adam's special formula, was used for delicately molded ornaments on mirrors and girandoles where wood would have been too brittle. The compo, while still plastic, was pressed into molds and left until it hardened, after which it could be applied by glue or panel pins to the surface to be decorated.

Adam provided designs at one time or another for practically every article of furnishing for the home. The articles made most frequently were chairs, stools, settees or sofas, window seats, day beds, bedsteads, tables, chests of drawers, console cabinets, secretaries, bookcases, mirrors, clocks, and sideboard tables flanked by pedestals holding urn-shaped cutlery boxes. It must be remembered that the Adam brothers were architects and designers, and not makers of furniture. When the term "Adam furniture" is used, it means furniture made directly from Adam designs, not by them.

George Hepplewhite and Thomas Sheraton

George Hepplewhite and Thomas Sheraton are two names that are outstanding in the consideration of furniture styles of the late eighteenth century. The work of both men has left a lasting imprint. Again the reason for this distinction is that they each published books of designs. George Hepplewhite died in 1786. In 1788, two years after his death, his wife, Alice, published a book of designs with the title page:

The Cabinet-Maker and Upholsterer's Guide; or, repository of designs for every article of household furniture, in the newest and most approved taste; displaying a great variety of patterns . . . In the plainest and most enriched styles; with a scale to each, and an explanation in letterpress. Also the plan of a room, showing the proper distribution of the furniture. The whole exhibiting near three hundred different designs, engraved on one hundred and twenty-six plates, from drawings by A. Hepplewhite and Co. Cabinet-Makers. London. Published by I. and J. Taylor . . . 1788.

In 1789 a second edition was published, with one additional plate and a few small alterations. "The third edition improved," which came out in 1794, contained another new plate and some substantial changes, mainly affecting designs for chairs.

The first book of designs by Thomas Sheraton (1751–1806) was probably published in forty-two separate numbers; the plates were dated from 1791 to 1793. The first complete edition was published in 1793 and 1794 under the title

The Cabinet-Maker and Upholsterer's Drawing Book. In Three Parts. By Thomas Sheraton, Cabinet-Maker. London. Printed for the author, by T. Bensley; and sold by J. Mathews, No. 18, Strand; G. Terry, No. 54 Paternoster-Row; J. S. Jordan, No. 166

Fleet Street, L. Wayland, Middle-Row, Holborn; and by the author No. 41, Davies Street, Grosvenor Square. (Engravers: G. Terry, J. Newton, J. Barlow, Thornwaite, J. J. Caldwell, J. Cooke and others.)

The Cabinet Maker's Dictionary followed in 1802, and in 1804 was begun *The Cabinet-Maker, Upholsterer and General Artists' Encyclopaedia*, which was never finished.

These two men may more accurately be called designer-publicists. There is no evidence in the form of bills or references to Hepplewhite in contemporary documents to suggest that as a cabinetmaker he enjoyed extensive or fashionable patronage. No articles of furniture have been identified with the firm, and the name of it does not appear in the London Directory. Little furniture corresponds exactly to the plates in the *Guide*. It is not even certain that he was the author of the designs. The absence of any reference to him on the title page and the interval of two years between his death and publication of the book suggest that another hand may have been responsible for part or all of the work.

Although it is known that Thomas Sheraton was reared as a cabinetmaker, it is doubtful that he set up a workshop of his own. He was an itinerant Baptist preacher, tractarian, drawing master, designer, and publisher. It is reputed that he would make friends with footmen in the fashionable houses and bribe them for permission to hide behind the draperies and make sketches of the furnishings. This is possible, since his books did not always show original designs but portrayed the popular taste of the time.

People have a natural tendency to place a name on everything. A customer enters an antique shop and in examining an article of furniture may read on the tag "English, c. 1790," and ask "Is it Hepplewhite or Sheraton?" In the majority of cases it cannot be designated as of one style or the other. The designs of the two men were closely parallel in so many respects that it is necessary to consider them jointly. Both followed Adam's footsteps in continuing in the neo-classical mood. They also belonged to the school of colorists. The Adam influence, with its severe lines and cold chaste ornament, affected both of them, but they shared a tendency for lightness and delicacy. They each had a sound appreciation of form and proportion. Hepplewhite, though his name was given to a style, was less original than his contemporaries, including Sheraton. His chief merit was that he successfully adapted the neo-classical style to ordinary household furniture, a quality shared by countless other, forgotten cabinetmakers. In many of the designs illustrated in the *Guide*, he contrived to impart to plain and useful objects a sober elegance that makes them ideal for modern homes. He contributed little that was new to the style introduced by Adam. His repertoire of ornament was confined to the usual neo-classical stock of urns, medallions, paterae, swags, pendants, and similar devices, which occur with frequency through all his work. Whereas Hepplewhite developed the use of satinwood and colored woods in inlaying tabletops, knife boxes, and tea caddies to a great extent, Sheraton in Anglicizing the French Louis XVI style used more carving and reeding. There is a good deal of lathework noticeable in the tapering legs that Hepplewhite drew for chairs, tables, and sideboards. Sheraton's legs were often turned, or turned and reeded. They both chose mahogany as the best wood for chairmaking. Hepplewhite introduced chairs with oval and heart-shaped backs disconnected from the seats. Three patterns most frequently used for his chair backs were the honeysuckle, an adaptation of the Greek design acclimatized by Adam; the Prince of Wales feathers; and the wheat ear. Sheraton, with his partiality to the straight line, designed square or rectangular chair backs disconnected from the seats, filled in with fretted panels, urns, or latticing or barring. The toprails were straight. These chairs would have either tapering legs with spade feet or, more often, turned or reeded legs. Sheraton had a mechanical ability that resulted in the invention of articles of an ingenious character. These were very popular in the late eighteenth century. He designed many functional pieces, such as a library table that concealed a stepladder for reaching the top shelves of a bookcase, folding bedsteads, couches that could be changed into tables, combined bookcases and washstands, gout stools that could be altered to various elevations. The most astonishing fancy was an ottoman with heating irons underneath, so that the seat might be kept at a proper temperature in cold weather.

There is necessarily a similarity in the listing of furniture in use in each period of the eighteenth century, since no revolutionary change took place in the living habits of the people. Certain pieces were discontinued from period to period or from style to style, and some new ones were introduced. By this time highboys and lowboys were no longer

SHERATON SIDEBOARD

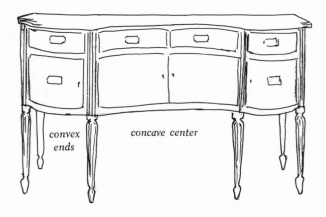

convex
ends

concave center

made. Taking the place of highboys were chests on chests and presses or wardrobes. More pretentious and elaborate dressing tables took the place of lowboys. Bookcases, cabinets, and sideboards became more important.

The sideboard with drawers and cupboards was introduced. Prior to this, Chippendale and Adam designed sideboard tables. It is now thought that the first design for a sideboard was in Thomas Shearer's book of designs, *The Cabinet-Makers' London Book of Prices*, which was published in 1788. But Hepplewhite and Sheraton quickly followed in the development of this useful addition to the household. It is illustrated in Hepplewhite's 1794 edition and in Sheraton's 1802 publication. Hepplewhite had a tendency to use a serpentine front with concave ends, whereas Sheraton used a bow front, or broken front with convex ends attached to rectilinear corners.

Sheraton's designs ushered in a type of dining table that solved the problem of interfering wooden legs. Instead of the drop-leaf table with four to six legs and demilune extensions, this new type of table was supported by a column or pedestal

HEPPLEWHITE SIDEBOARD

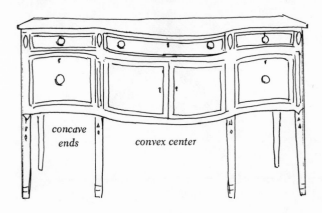

concave ends

convex center

at each end, which rested on four feet that splayed outward. In the case of additional ends they, too, were supported on pedestal bases. Frequently these pedestals were urn-shaped and the splay legs were reeded and had brass claw feet.

When furniture is referred to as Hepplewhite or Sheraton, it simply means furniture of the type to which in the course of years their names have become attached. The Hepplewhite and Sheraton styles (not periods) enjoyed great favor

Sheraton-style tilt-top pedestal supper table,
English, circa 1815. Mahogany with rosewood banding,
four reeded curule legs terminating in brass feet
and casters attached to the pedestal.

*Sheraton and Hepplewhite chairs
showing the characteristic differences
between the two styles.*
LEFT: *English Sheraton, circa 1810.
Mahogany, an indented band to the straight crest rail,
carved feather center splat, fluted uprights,
tapered and turned legs. The stretcher is a later addition.*
RIGHT: *American Hepplewhite, circa 1800. Mahogany,
shield back, fluted tapering legs with spade feet.*

and vogue, and exerted a powerful and lasting effect upon
English and American furniture.

Early Federal Period, 1776–1800

"Now the Revolution is won, the style of Chippendale is done" ran the couplet, and, in fact, after the Revolution the classic revival style introduced into England by Robert Adam did sweep aside the rococo in the new republic. The classic style is called Federal or Republic in America, and the architecture of the young country was influenced by it to a great extent. The cabinetmakers, however, were not swayed to the same degree. The books of Hepplewhite and Sheraton and Shearer's *Cabinet-Makers' London Book of Prices* circulated the current styles of London in the United States and provided models of form and ornament. Although American furniture was derived from English furniture, there were many subtle differences. There was a similarity of parts, but they were combined in various ways and proportions according to individual interpretations and the needs of the purchasers.

Traits and styles of living in each location played an important part in the furniture constructed in America. The wealthier, more sophisticated centers such as Boston, Newport, New York, Philadelphia, Baltimore, and Charleston produced furniture of the highest quality and standard. In more remote or provincial areas, where homes and fashions were simpler, less ornate furniture was produced. The availability of woods was an important factor in what the cabinetmaker used in the construction of furniture. Cabinetmakers near the Atlantic Coast or a waterway used mahogany almost exclusively for the primary wood. Quantities of mahogany were being shipped into the Atlantic ports from the West Indies, and because of the ease of shipping, it proved an inexpensive wood and so became much used. Inland settlements in the 1790s and early 1800s used locally grown woods

Sheraton-style clover-leaf card table, circa 1810.
Mahogany turned and fluted legs, brass ball feet.
A style adopted by Duncan Phyfe.

for the primary parts of the furniture; examples are native walnut in Pennsylvania, and wild cherry in Connecticut, especially throughout the Connecticut River Valley. Secondary woods (those used on the parts of a piece of furniture

Hepplewhite-style hunt board, American, circa 1815,
a form generally in use throughout the South.
Pecan, showing the use of a locally grown wood,
fitted with drawers, bottle drawers, and cupboards
(with replaced hardware), tapering legs.

that do not show) were chosen from the woods found more
abundantly in the locale in which the individual cabinetmaker was working. It is possible for a connoisseur to identify

just where an article of furniture was made from the woods that were used to make it.

In America after 1790, veneers and decorative inlays of many kinds were a principal method of ornamenting furniture. (Use was scanty between 1760 and 1790.) Pictorial inlays such as shells, flowers, and eagles were inset to provide points of interest and contrast. Light and dark inlaid lines, called stringing, were used, often in patterns of diamonds and checkers (see Hepplewhite-style card table in the color section, following p. 114).

Every well-populated section had its trained cabinet-makers. The names of many of these important craftsmen are known at the present time. Awareness of them has come from advertisements in newspapers, documents, and bills of sale. Very occasionally, a signed or labeled piece of furniture is located. This is a windfall. With close scrutiny of the

AMERICAN FEDERAL INLAY DESIGNS

eagle with shield

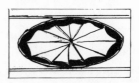

bellflower

sunburst

Hepplewhite-style bow-front bureau, American,
made in the South, circa 1800.
Mahogany, original oval brasses, shaped apron, splay feet.

cabinetwork, it can be learned how a particular man worked, and through this observation other articles made by him can be identified. It takes years of training and collecting data on the woods used in certain sections and the idiosyncrasies of individual craftsmen to arrive at this level. There are a number of erudite books and articles (see Bibliography) on outstanding cabinetmakers of New England, New York, Philadelphia, Charleston, Savannah, and other locations where furniture was produced in eighteenth- and nineteenth-century America, which can be most advantageous to

Fancy Sheraton-style bench,
painted with a stencil design, American, circa 1820.
Turned legs joined by stretchers.

the fairly recent collector when he has arrived at the state of
wanting to know where certain pieces of furniture were
made and, if possible, by whom.

In studying antique furniture, it is important to keep in
mind that basic forms continued to be made over long periods. New forms and fashions appeared rapidly between 1780
and 1825 in America, but the old ones lingered on for as
long as twenty to fifty years (see color section, following p.
114). This can be seen in new and revised editions of price
books. Even as late as 1860, price books printed in London
continued to illustrate furniture in what is now known as

Hepplewhite and Sheraton styles. As families moved westward, they had new furniture made in the styles they were accustomed to using, or from examples they had carried with them. All of these factors must be taken into consideration in dating articles of American furniture in the Federal style.

VI

Early Nineteenth Century
The English Regency Period
1800-1830

The Prince of Wales ruled as Prince Regent throughout the time of the illness of his father (George III), from 1811 until 1820, but the term Regency is given to the decorative-arts style that flourished during the first thirty years of the nineteenth century (at one time called English Empire). It was an age with contrasting qualities of grace, simplicity, elegance, robustness, and splendor. The style did not reflect the personal extravagant grandeur of the Prince.

The nineteenth century saw the beginning of the industrial era. Domestic craftsmen were superseded by specialized laborers and graded technicians, who organized into larger industries. Craftwork was becoming more and more mechan-

English Regency armchair, circa 1805.
Mahogany with brass inlay,
rope-carved crest rail and back, uprights, scimitar legs.

ical. There developed a prejudice against the handmade object in the flourishing, ever-increasing middle class. By the 1790s, woodworking machinery had been invented and a patent for a mechanical planing machine had been issued. Sawing, grooving, mortising, rebating, molding, and other elementary processes were influenced by this latter invention. Not all woodworking was taken over by the new machines, but they were frequently used for reducing expense. The economic situation also affected trends in design. From 1795 to 1820, the period of the Napoleonic Wars and their aftermath, the cost of living doubled in England, and the demand for complicated and more expensive woodwork lessened.

Sheraton's book of designs published during the early years of the century was extremely popular. French Empire styles were in fashion, with Nelson as hero in place of Napoleon. The Nelsoniana craze, with naval associations, anchors, cannons, cables, and so on, was the genesis of some of Sheraton's designs, including "Nelson's chairs" with arc back, rounded knees, and scimitar legs.

In 1807, shortly after Sheraton's death, a book of designs entitled *Household Furniture and Interior Decoration* was published by the scholar and architect Thomas Hope (1770–1831). Hope had studied architecture in Greece, Egypt, Turkey, and Syria, and was the owner of a large collection of antiquities. His interests were predominantly archaeological and his furniture was from these classical sources. He was greatly influenced by the motifs on Greek pottery. There was also a strong Egyptian trend in furniture design, inspired both by Napoleon's campaign in Egypt in 1798 and by Vivant Denon's book *Voyages dans la basse et haute Egypte*. And there was a limited revival of chinoiserie. The use of japanning returned to favor.

Mahogany, elm, oak, beech, walnut, pine, and rosewood

were all used for furniture-making at this time; however, mahogany, beech, and rosewood were used more extensively. Mahogany has never ceased to be used for surface wood from the time of its introduction in the second quarter of the eighteenth century. After 1790, the supply of the dark, madder-colored mahogany from Honduras diminished and its place was given over to Cuban (or Spanish mahogany, as it was called), characterized by a lighter tone and a brownish color fading to a tawny yellow. By 1810, veneers of the Cuban mahogany, which displayed handsome markings, including crotch, swirl, plum-pudding, blister, stripe, or roe figures, were used more often to decorate the surfaces of furniture. These vivid veneers were used until about 1830.

Rosewood came into use late in the eighteenth century, first for bands of inlay. From 1800 on, it was used for surfacing oak or mahogany carcasses, and on pine for simpler pieces. Small articles were occasionally made up completely of rosewood. With the neo-rococo revival after the Great Exhibition at the Crystal Palace in London in 1851, rosewood was used less, since it did not lend itself to the semi-mechanical carving of the Victorian era.

Walnut, which had been used so extensively from the days of Charles II to the time of George I, reappeared in the 1830s.

Elm was employed, especially for so-called farmhouse or country furniture, as was beech. London makers, however, made furniture of beech and grained it to simulate rosewood, or japanned it black. It was also painted in various colors, as well as gilded.

Satinwood, which had been used in the earlier years of the Adam period, was a hangover from the 1790s. This inspired the use of other sensational yellow or yellowish woods, such as zebrawood and calamander. Maple—plain, bird's-eye, and curly—was used from before 1820 into the third quarter

English Regency sofa table, circa 1815.
Mahogany, drop leaves and drawers, end supports,
scimitar legs terminating in brass collars and casters.

of the century as a substitute for satinwood.

Inlays consisted of ebony—sometimes replaced by black-stained pear wood—white holly, and satinwood. Ivory and silver were inset in the more important furniture. Inlaid decorations of brass were characteristic of surface adornment on Regency furniture.

The usual articles of furniture continued to be made, but

new types appeared as well. Among these were: the whatnot, a portable open stand with four uprights enclosing shelves for books and ornaments; and the music Canterbury, a small stand usually mounted on casters, with partitions for music books and sometimes small drawers for sheets of music. The supper Canterbury was introduced as an accessory piece in the dining room, also intended for use when servants were not present. Sheraton wrote that it "held knives, forks, and plates at that end, which is made circular on purpose." The fire or pole screen, necessary to give protection from the intense heat of open fires, was not a novelty, but at this time it underwent two distinct changes: the former tripod base gave way to a solid base, and the screen took the form of a banner hung from a bar on an upright. The teapoy, a small three- or four-legged table or stand, was also in use in drawing rooms at this time. This custom fitted the taste of well-to-do people, who considered it stylish and convenient to place various small occasional tables—such as rectangular stands with end supports, little worktables, and sets or nests of three or four tables—about the room. The sofa table was in great demand from the first years of the nineteenth century. Its convenient size and form made it a desirable article for the parlor, drawing room, or library. As the name implies, it was designed to be placed in front of a sofa and was intended to provide a reading or writing spot for anyone sitting on the sofa. These tables measured about five feet in length and two feet in width, and were constructed with two ornamental end supports, which were joined by a horizontal stretcher rail or supported on a central pedestal mounted on a platform with splayed feet.

Toward the end of the Regency period there was a deterioration in the standards of furniture-making in all but the finest pieces, which heralded the decline that took place in the Early Victorian era.

American Empire parlor chair, circa 1820.
Mahogany, volute carved crest rail and slat,
slip seat, scimitar legs.

American Federal and Empire, 1800–1845

Neo-classical influence continued in America during the first half of the nineteenth century. The furniture of this period is referred to as Federal or Empire, depending upon the predominance of characteristics from English or French sources. The classic revival in America may be loosely divided into three periods. The Early Federal, from 1776 to 1800, has been discussed previously. The Late Federal can be fixed roughly from 1800 to 1825. At this time, American furniture continued to show the influence of Sheraton's designs, as well as other English Regency forms, but around 1820 it began to reveal a distinct divergence from English traditions. The klismos and curule chairs, the use of animal supports as well as archaeological forms derived not only from the Regency but also from the Greco-Roman and Egyptian influences so popular in France during the Directoire and Consulate (1795–1804) and the Empire (1804–1815) periods. There appeared a profusion of heavy, deep carving or roped reeding, acanthus leaves, plumes, diamond-patterned pineapple motifs, and large animal paw feet with hairy shanks (see color section, following p. 114). The third and final phase of the neo-classical influence in the United States was roughly from 1825 to 1845. Furniture during this time was closely related to the architectural style known as Greek Revival. By the late 1830s, the foregoing designs had been superseded by this

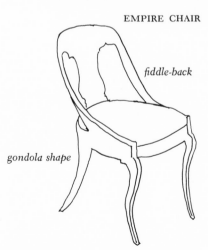

EMPIRE CHAIR

fiddle-back

gondola shape

American Federal grouping.
Sheraton-style gilt mirror, New York, circa 1810,
with original églomisé (painted glass) panel,
surmounted by a spread eagle and side finials.
A New York card table, circa 1815.
Mahogany, supported by four uprights rising from the platform,
four carved and gilded acanthus-kneed legs with claw feet.

style, with its simple lines, planed surfaces, and extensive use of massive pillars or columns and scroll uprights and feet.

Baltimore produced the richest interpretations of London fashions—caned-and-painted seating furniture (see color section, following p. 114) and highly inlaid cabinetwork. A number of very skillful cabinetmakers had emigrated to Maryland from England soon after the Revolution, and continued working in the English manner. The most distinctive element of Maryland's Federal style was the use of reverse painted glass (églomisé) panels, inset in bookcases, desks, and tables.

From the beginning of the nineteenth century, New York City was the leader in high-style cabinetmaking. There were many excellent cabinetmakers, but the one whose name is most familiar is Duncan Phyfe. Phyfe practiced cabinetmaking in New York from 1792 until his retirement in 1847, a period of fifty-five years. The best of Phyfe furniture is that for which he himself was responsible; i.e., the furniture produced in the last years of the eighteenth century and during the first quarter of the nineteenth century. In successive years, he employed more than a hundred journeymen, including cabinetmakers, turners, and carvers. His shop eventually evolved in assembly-line method patterned after one developed in Philadelphia in the 1820s, which distributed the labor among skilled and less skilled workers, the skilled doing the specialized work while the less skilled did the simpler tasks. It is important to note, however, that, unlike later methods, this was not a factory procedure with power-driven machinery. The early work, which was done primarily by Phyfe himself, accounts for the approach to perfection of some of his pieces. His patrons were the well-to-do, not only in New York but in thriving centers along the Eastern seaboard and in the South, where he had warehouses to supply his customers. He charged, and received, top prices for his furniture, and was able to produce the best.

Phyfe profited from the study and experience of the great

English and French cabinetmakers and designers of the late eighteenth century. Their methods, manner of construction, and decoration appealed to him, and from them he created a style of his own. The work of Phyfe and his contemporary craftsmen marked an end of the era of good taste, which vanished with the industrial revolution later in the nineteenth century. There were other well-known skilled early-nineteenth-century cabinetmakers. Among them were Charles-Honoré Lannuier, New York's Parisian immigrant cabinetmaker; Michael Allison, also of New York; Henry Connelly, Ephraim Haines, and Joseph B. Barry, working in Philadelphia; Samuel McIntire and Thomas Seymour, of Salem, Massachusetts. It is the name of Phyfe, however, that stands out prominently. Even the neophyte has a rudimentary acquaintance with some of Phyfe's forms of furniture and the diverse details of his carved ornaments, since they have been reproduced continually over the years in fine furniture as well as inexpensive copies. A popular table of Phyfe design was the drop leaf with carved urn-shaped pedestal, terminating in four saber legs supporting a clover-

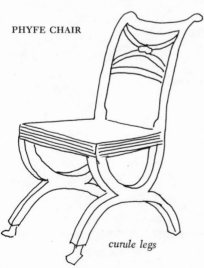

PHYFE CHAIR

curule legs

leaf-shaped top. He also made card tables and Pembroke tables with tapering, fluted legs, in the manner of Sheraton. Other forms identified with Phyfe were chairs and settees with a curule or Roman base; chairs with a lyre splat; the Grecian or Recamier couch with scrolled ends; and cabinet pieces with the Egyptian animal leg and foot. The sofas had upholstered arms, back, and seat, or were caned. The back panels in sofas and chairs showed many variations of ornament. Among the decorative methods in the carving were: the acanthus leaf; the water leaf; the dog's foot, used to terminate the front legs of benches, chairs, and tables; the lion's foot with eagle wing; rosettes; fluting; lion mask; cornucopia; laurel; drapery swags; wheat ears; thunderbolt; Prince of Wales feathers; and the lyre. These were used singly or in combination.

Phyfe was both a chairmaker and a cabinetmaker. He preferred the lighter forms of furniture related in construction to chairmaking rather than the heavier cabinetwork. His chief output comprised chairs, tables, and sofas, but he made many other miscellaneous articles for special purposes. The finest quality of mahogany was always used, even during the second and third quarters of the century when the furniture became large and unwieldy.

The furniture of Phyfe and his talented contemporaries reflects the new American taste and culture, a civilization soon to decline as the century progressed. It is all much sought after and highly valuable.

PHYFE DECORATIONS

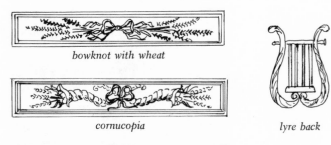

bowknot with wheat

cornucopia

lyre back

swag with bowknot and tassel

VII

Victorian Furniture
1835-1910

The Georgian era ended in 1830 with the death of George IV. The house of Hanover had held the throne in England continually since George I came to rule in 1714. William IV became king in 1830, but for only seven years, at which time Queen Victoria began her long reign. The Victorian period can be said to have started, roughly, around 1835, when the Georgian order began to vanish. It had completely disappeared by the end of the 1840s. For all practical purposes, then, the Victorian era began during the reign of William IV (1830–1837), continued strong during Victoria's rule (1837–1901), and lasted through the years of Edward VII (1901–1910). Art Nouveau, a style introduced about 1885 to counteract the mass production of the industrial age, must also be included in this long span.

The Victorian style was a new way of life. Industrial design was the order of the day; design meant decoration, and in decoration the Victorians proved to be the most exhaustive elaborators. With the Victorians there developed an eclecticism of taste based on historical revivals, including the Gothic, rococo, Elizabethan, French Louis XV, and Louis XVI. Actually there was no design presented without an attribution to some historical time. In the 1830s, when this eclecticism took over, there resulted a consistent and distinct Early Victorian style of household furnishings. The most popular of all the revival styles appearing in the mid-nineteenth century was the rococo. Although the same features were used as in the eighteenth-century rococo—the cabriole leg, curvilinear surfaces, S curves and scrolls, and shell carving—there were significant differences that distorted the revival pieces. The cabriole leg would sometimes terminate in an S-scroll toe, or in a straight cylinder. The rear leg, instead of being cabriole in the true Louis XV fashion, was formed of a reverse curve chamfered at the termination to give a sense of solidity to the piece. Scrolls were interpreted in a heavier manner, and the naturalistic carving of flowers, fruits, and birds gave an exuberant lacy quality when it was incorporated into the overall design of the piece.

The chief characteristic of Elizabethan Revival was the

VICTORIAN TABLE   BALL-AND-TWIST TURNING

scroll-support card table

QUATREFOIL

use of the ball-and-spiral twist turning, which was actually
an adaptation from a style popular in the time of Charles I
and Charles II. By some inexplicable quirk, the revivalists
mistook this for a design typical of the sixteenth century. The
majority of chairs in this trend are usually of walnut, tall-
backed, short-legged, low-seated, with an entirely upholstered back and seat. These chairs were called devotional,
prie-dieu, or vesper chairs. Another baroque decorative device from this influence was the application of split spindles
to the front of cabinet pieces. The Gothic Revival was not by
any means introduced for the first time. Since its beginning
in medieval times, each succeeding age turned to it in some
degree for inspiration, and there were always some devotees.
Horace Walpole's house, Strawberry Hill, was built in the
"Gothick" manner about 1750. At times, Gothic Revival
was used in conjunction with other influences, and usually
was restricted to the hall furnishings. It was followed much
less in the United States than in Europe, since there were no
crenelated ruins in the States to stimulate interest. The chief
motifs emphasized in Gothic furniture were pointed and
lancet arches, rosettes, heraldic devices, crockets, trefoils,
finials, and tracery. These were mainly seen, especially in
American furniture, in chairs, cabinet pieces, and beds.

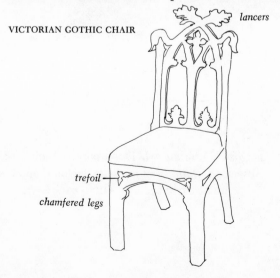

VICTORIAN GOTHIC CHAIR

lancers

trefoil

chamfered legs

English Victorian-style Davenport desk, circa 1845.
Rosewood, spiral twist uprights, melon-shaped feet,
drawers on the side with a trick lock.

Victorian furniture was solid and well made, suggestive of commercial prosperity. The workmanship was usually first-class and the wood generally of good quality. The popular primary woods were mahogany, rosewood, and walnut. Oak was used briefly at the end of the century. The secondary woods were apt to be pines of various sorts, and poplar.

Now everything was judged by realistic standards. Carving was realistic. Ornament was not appreciated unless it blazoned forth and covered all visible surfaces. This crowded decoration did nothing to tie the design together but, on the contrary, obstructed all unity. There was emphasis on comfort rather than style. This was evident by 1850 in the design of sofas, couches, and ottomans. A wooden framework was visible in the back and arms of the sofas. The single-, double-, or even triple-humped back often incorporated carved or fretwork panels. There was an increased use of upholstery and padding, which merged separate parts of each piece of stuffed furniture into a unified whole, arms and backs joined together in a single enclosing sweep. The variant settee, known as the sociable, the conversation sofa, or the tête-à-tête, was introduced, making it possible for two people to sit side by side but facing each other. A significant change in

VICTORIAN TÊTE-À-TÊTE

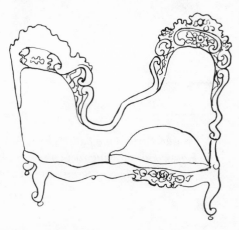

Victorian Belter-type parlor chair, American, circa 1850.
Rosewood, showing rococo revival, laminated back,
cabriole legs terminating in scroll feet.

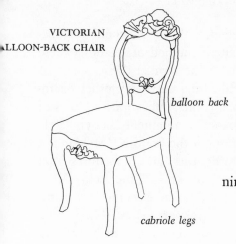

VICTORIAN
BALLOON-BACK CHAIR

balloon back

cabriole legs

chair design was the development of the balloon back, which became the most common type of construction in various chairs for the dining room and the drawing room. In America, by the mid-nineteenth century, a number of factors in furniture were changing. The furniture-making centers were still largely in the major cities of the Eastern seaboard. At the time of the Crystal Palace Exhibition in London in 1851, New York continued to be the leader in both style and production. But in the 1840s there was a large influx of German carvers and cabinetmakers, who brought with them a different training and outlook; in addition, a number of French cabinetmakers emigrated to America. Although they were far outnumbered by the Germans, the French dominated the fine furniture trade of the 1850s and set the style for several decades. It was, however, the German-born John Henry Belter (1804–1863) who became the best known of America's mid-century cabinetmakers. His name stands out as a cabinetmaker of importance in the 1840s in the way Duncan Phyfe's did in the early part of the century. Belter was renowned for his laminated and carved rococo-revival rosewood parlor-and-bedroom suites. The principle of lamination was not a new one; the Egyptians were aware of it and constructed the tops of sarcophagi from panels of laminated wood. Belter's process consisted of gluing together thin layers of wood—rosewood, oak, ebonized hardwood—about a sixteenth of an inch thick, so that the grain of a given layer ran in the opposite direction from that on either side. The average number of layers was from six to eight, although it could vary between three and sixteen. Belter's method of steaming these panels in molds—or "cawls," as he termed them—made it possible to achieve great undulating curves. Another distinguishing feature of his work was the application of pieces of solid wood to the frame for extra ornament. Belter's style went from the looseness of form of the Louis XV style in the late 1840s and early 1850s to tightness and shapeliness from the mid-1850s until his death, at which time Louis XIV, Louis XVI, and Renaissance styles had become dominant. Few signed pieces of Belter furniture are extant. There were, however, imitators of Belter who were active in New York and other cities at the time. Among the more prominent were Charles A. Baudoine, of New York, and George Henkels, of Philadelphia, both working in laminated furniture. Other important rococo-revival cabinetmakers in America were August Jansen, the Meeks brothers, Alexander Roux, Leon Marcotte, and Gustave Herter, in New York; Daniel Pabst and Gottlieb Volmer, in Philadelphia; François Seignoret and Prudent Mallard, in New Orleans; and S. S. Johns, in Cincinnati.

The year of Queen Victoria's birth, 1819, is generally considered the beginning of the industrial age in England and America. However, even in the eighteenth century, an expanding and wealthier population was demanding more and more goods, which could not be produced by the early factories fueled by wood and powered by water and wind. Coal came to replace wood, and early-model steam engines were introduced to drain water and raise coal from the earth. The badge of the industrial revolution is the use of steam for power and the greatly improved engine (1769) by James Watt. And, of course, more products became available because of mass production.

As early as the latter half of the eighteenth century, factors that made possible the industrial revolution were present in the cabinetmakers' trade. But the thrust of the revolution did not make itself felt until after 1800, and even then development was slow. The major changes in American furniture-making were the mass production of clock parts by Eli Terry and chair parts by Lambert Hitchcock, both in Connecticut; the harnessing of water power for the sawing of lumber and veneers; and the increased specialization of workmen in the production of individual parts. Improvements in the saw, more than any other tool, placed furniture under the domination of the machine. The circular saw was known during the eighteenth century but not until the 1840s did it come into widespread use. The advantage of this saw was that it could make very fine cuts, and thus thinner and larger sheets of veneer could be made with it. It became possible to produce enormous veneered surfaces to cover a soft secondary wood in large pieces of cabinet furniture. The development of the band saw was not so rapid; not until the 1850s was a satisfactory form of construction discovered. Wood-carving machines, fret-cutting machines, and planing and mortising machines were developed and refined again and again before the end of the century, each responsible in part for the quantities of inexpensive and ill-designed furniture turned out during the latter half of the century.

By the 1830s and 1840s, the use of power machines in the larger establishments became the norm, although, of course, machines did not appear everywhere at once. Small cabinetmakers in the rural areas continued to make acceptable handmade furniture long after 1830, whereas prominent urban firms, such as Duncan Phyfe in New York, were beginning to use machinery to some extent prior to 1820. It is difficult to fix a rigid date line between antique and just old. You should always take into consideration how a piece is made as well as when. Hitchcock chairs were in production before 1830, yet all their parts were machine-made, almost in assembly-line fashion. Consequently they are not antique in the sense that a true antique must be the handmade product of an individual craftsman or a group of craftsmen and not a piece that came out of a machine. In contrast, the pine furniture and slat-back chairs made by the Shakers may date as late as 1850, but each piece is individually made and reflects the sociological and religious beliefs of its makers. There is no hesitancy in referring to this furniture as antique, and it is priced accordingly—high. In the late 1850s the Shaker factory in New Lebanon, New York, became increasingly organized and production was greatly expanded. These later, machine-made Shaker chairs are not antique.

Machinery almost destroyed the art of the craftsman. It brought about a complete breakdown in the guild or apprentice system of craftsmanship, because the need for handwork disappeared as mechanized equipment took over the work of the individual. A single object, instead of being visualized and created by one person, became mass-produced by a number of workers. More and more elaborate products were derived from power-driven machines, and the competitive spirit that produced them was displayed in the Great Exhibition of 1851 at the Crystal Palace in London and the Exposition in New York in 1853. Furniture was bulky and covered with flat pattern and applied ornament. Decorative motifs were taken from many historical sources and used in indiscriminate combinations, disregarding the original purpose.

To combat the excesses of mid-century revivals and the decline of the quality of ornament caused by mechanization, English designers such as William Morris and Bruce Talbert and their followers urged reform and pioneered the arts-and-crafts movement. Morris had been trained in architecture, but he turned to furniture design in 1861, when he founded a company to offer the public furniture in good taste. Morris and his associates used the English Gothic of the thirteenth century for inspiration, but were more concerned with its basic structure, line, and proportions than copying the Gothic ornament exactly. The furniture produced by the Morris firm was constructed and decorated completely by hand, which resulted, of course, in objects too costly for popular consumption.

Morris's chief apostle in England and America was Charles Lock Eastlake, whose book *Hints on Household Taste*, published in England in 1868 and followed by eight American editions from 1872 to 1890, had as much influence on the household furnishings of his time as Sheraton's and Hepplewhite's had had in theirs. Eastlake was opposed to revival styles and promoted furniture that was simple, straightforward, and Early English in its style inspiration. It was made of oak and had simple and incised decoration.

The arts-and-crafts movement flourished from 1882 to 1910. Guilds for craftsmen were formed in England to encourage the creation and exhibition of objects that put materials and workmanship to proper use. This movement turned to humble, handmade things, and brought a revival of cottage crafts. In the United States it was not so thoroughly organized as it was in England.

By the middle of Victoria's reign, Indian teakwood furniture was being imported, and its artistic design produced a highly picturesque decorative effect. Sandalwood boxes and jewel caskets also lightened the appearance of many rooms. A taste for the Japanese evolved in the 1860s, because of the Japanese prints and textiles that were shown in the London Exposition of 1862 and the Paris Exposition of 1867. The furniture designed in this manner had very thin horizontal and vertical members, and cabinet pieces contained complicated shelf arrangements.

Metal furniture, too, was made and used during this time.

It falls into two categories. The first comprises cast-iron garden furniture and hall furniture such as hat-and-umbrella stands and flower stands. These were made as a by-product of the normal industrial work of the iron foundries in Coalbrookdale, Shropshire, and the smaller foundries in the Birmingham area. Cast iron was in production before 1830, but was particularly popular between 1845 and 1855. Coalbrookdale produced a complete assortment of indoor cast-iron furniture, including pieces for the living room upholstered in damask or velvet. Cast-iron furniture was made from an assemblage of parts cast in individual molds. The form that has survived in greatest quantities today is the garden bench, which often combined a wooden seat with an iron frame. In some cases, a firm that produced iron furniture made pieces from wire. The new wire-making machines made it possible to form this highly adaptable material into elaborate and fanciful shapes for chairs and plant stands, usually intended for outdoor use.

VICTORIAN
HAT-AND-
UMBRELLA
STAND

cast iron

The second category of metal furniture consists of brass. In 1825 the brass foundries of Birmingham had added beds to their normal output of cornice poles, fenders, and the like, but they made no real impact until 1844, when a report in the *Art Union* of the novelty of French metal furniture shown at the Paris Exhibition of 1844 seemed to boost their desirability. At the Great Exhibition in London in 1851, a variety of brass furniture was shown made from drawn-brass tubing, a comparatively new mechanical advance to which cast-brass ornaments were added, and brass furniture became a fashion. Brass beds continued in high style into the early years of the twentieth century.

Papier-mâché furniture comes to mind when one thinks of furnishings of the Victorian times, since it always seems to be included in settings of Victoriana. Although the material was invented in France many years before, it first came to England in the 1670s, when it was principally employed for making imitation stucco and plaster ceiling ornaments. At the end of the eighteenth century, a type of papier-mâché was patented that could subsequently be japanned and varnished. The lacquer colors used were black, red, and green. Mother-of-pearl was added to the repertoire about 1825, and reached its height of popularity before 1840. In 1847 the art of "gem inlaying" was patented. During the latter half of the nineteenth century, almost every sort of thing was made in papier-mâché, from small boxes and teapots to fire screens, chairs, settees, footstools, tables, beds, and even cabinets and secretaries. In America, the Litchfield Manufacturing Company, founded in 1850, made papier-mâché screens, boxes, small tables, and especially clock cases.

Andrew Jackson Downing (1815–1854), horticulturist, rural architect, and landscape gardener, was an arbiter of fashion in mid-nineteenth-century America. In his book *Architecture of Country Houses*, published in 1850, he illustrated furniture in the revival styles. Besides the so-called Elizabethan chairs with upholstered tall backs and low seats, described earlier, he illustrated many revival styles that were combined into single sets of what he termed "cottage furniture." This was simple mass-produced furniture made in softwood, painted and decorated, but with the spiral twist reduced to a ball-and-spool-turned straight member. Bedroom sets were predominant, decorated in the rococo taste, usually in classical shapes but with additions of some objects with Elizabethan and baroque devices, such as applications of split spindles down the front sides of bureaus or other cabinet pieces. Spool beds are cottage furniture; some were constructed of more refined wood, such as walnut or cherry, and left unpainted. Nests of tables, made of mahogany and rosewood and also unpainted, with spool-turned legs, were popular. Étagères or whatnots were made with split spindles or spool uprights, and were especially suitable to house the many ceramic knickknacks and souvenirs so dear to the heart of the Victorian.

In contrast to the furniture described above, Downing in his *Cottage Residences* (New York, 1844) illustrated a rustic garden bench and stated, "rustic seats placed here and there in the most inviting spots, will heighten the charm and enable us to enjoy at leisure the quiet beauty around." Remarks such as this stimulated the making of furniture from organic materials and principally by hand. Especially popular were articles fashioned from rustic wood; tree branches and roots were combined to form a natural seat or table. This was a furniture form that could be produced by anyone with a little imagination and a few tools.

Before closing discussion of the various types of furniture made during the latter half of the nineteenth century, mention must be made of the Renaissance-style furniture that was popularized

VICTORIAN RUSTIC TABLE

by Grand Rapids, Michigan. Machine-made interpretations were produced in enormous quantities, with heavy and flattened elements of design cheapening the product. An imposing bedroom suite of this type was made by the Berkey & Gay Company, of Grand Rapids, and displayed at the Centennial Exposition in Philadelphia in 1876. The display stimulated enormous interest in refurbishing bedrooms all over the country.

With the increasing scarcity and expense of good eighteenth- and early-nineteenth-century furniture, more and more people are turning to the furniture of the Victorian period to equip their homes. Until recently, all Victorian items were frowned upon and dismissed as not worthy to be considered as collectibles. However, the attention focused on the period in the past few years has changed this opinion. The exhibition in celebration of the hundredth anniversary of the Metropolitan Museum of Art in New York, April 16–September 7, 1970, titled 19th Century America, Furniture and Other Decorative Arts, attracted special awareness to the Victorian period. More and more people are buying houses built during the latter half of the nineteenth century and the early years of the twentieth century because of their spaciousness, superior construction, and price, and are restoring them to their former livability. This has been encouraged by the many historic preservation societies.

As has been shown above, there is a diversified choice of Victorian furniture that makes it possible for anyone to find something that will fit into any size house or any way of living. What can be considered the best buys? Pieces that have the least demand are the large, mahogany-veneered pieces made during the early years of the period: large chests of drawers with ogee or sleigh fronts, wardrobes, and heavy carved sofas. They are too big to fit into the average newly built house with low ceilings, and are consequently priced low. However, they are ideal for the high-ceilinged, large-room houses of the third quarter of the century, and should be considered not only from the price angle but also because they are of good construction and made of handsome crotch-mahogany veneer. Many pieces in the revival styles—Elizabethan, Renaissance, and Gothic—can be included in the category of large furniture that is in a lower price range. Their massiveness and exuberant carving often make them less desirable than other pieces, but some of this can be camouflaged by lightening the upholstered areas with a bright, cheery chintz, or even by painting the wood a light color.

For the smaller Victorian house there is the cottage furniture in natural or painted pine. This was machine-made in enormous quantities, not only for home consumption but for use in many summer hotels where it was employed almost entirely to equip the bedrooms. The hotels are being vacated and dismantled rapidly and cottage furniture has been appearing on the market in recent years at reasonable prices. It was never intended to be sophisticated or pretentious, but it has simplicity and, usually, good lines, and is pleasing. A number of people have been swayed by the current fashion and popularity of the later wicker and lacquered bamboo furniture, and have used it to furnish their end-of-the-century small houses. It has received such acclaim recently that it is being vastly reproduced and is selling at unrealistically steep prices. Remember it is to your advantage to buy the objects that are not as popular or in such great demand.

Art Nouveau and Art Deco have been the recipients of excessive attention, causing the prices to rise prohibitively and making anything in that class out of bounds for anyone but the serious, affluent collector. Nevertheless, it is good to be aware of it and to be able to recognize it: one never knows when an article will be placed on sale unknowingly.

Inasmuch as a considerable number of shops carry factory-made furniture of the early years of the twentieth century, a warning should again be directed to the prospective buyer. Much of this furniture is poorly constructed, poorly designed, and made of inferior wood. The only reason to purchase it is if it can be obtained cheaply. There is no resale possibility for it. It is far better to buy the moderately priced furniture mentioned above. If this is bought at a reasonable price, it can be disposed of without a loss, and in many cases at a gain, as your taste matures or changes.

ART NOUVEAU CHAIR

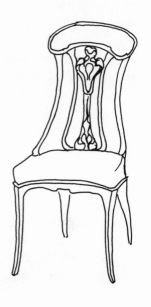

ART NOUVEAU SCREEN

VIII

Take a Second Look

A couple who had shown a desire for antiques, and had read, studied, and taken an interest in museums, restored a fine old house in a historic district, sparing no expense. The wife thought that with her knowledge she could certainly find good things at a bargain. After the house was completely restored and furnished, she called in an appraiser to inventory and value their "irreplaceables" for insurance. The appraiser on first entering the house was pleasantly impressed with the general appearance of taste and charm. But what a reversal of opinion upon closer examination! Was that new top on a tilt-top table from a packing box, as the lettering that could be seen clearly on the bottom indicated? Further, the pedestal was adapted from a fire-screen pole. Nearby was a candlestand with a reconstructed birdcage support added to attempt to raise the value. The most blatant fraud was the completely rebuilt secretary-bookcase. The Chippendale-style base was the only original part, and any value it might have had had been destroyed when the large chamfered legs had been cut down. The desk section was entirely new.

The owner was not as disturbed as she might have been; since she is an intelligent person, she was tremendously interested, and carefully watched what the appraiser was checking, asking many questions. She wanted to make no mistakes in her future buying. Fortunately there were some good pieces in the house as well. Her downfall was in trying to find bargains. She had access to an "importing house," where she could purchase wholesale. Although these pieces turned out to be junk, she did not feel the experience was a total loss, for she had learned a valuable lesson.

Plenty of good antique furniture is still available and there is certainly no dearth of antique shops. They pop up everywhere overnight like toadstools after a rain, clustered together in urban areas (to attract maximum interest), in every village and crossroad, at malls, flea markets, and similar vendues. With the interest in antiques growing constantly, many people think opening an antique shop is a quick and easy way to turn a dollar, and often little consideration is given to how knowledgeable they are of the subject. There are, fortunately, excellent shops that handle authentic antiques of all sorts in all price ranges whose owners are extremely well informed and will instruct the customer on what to look for in examining furniture and will continue to aid him in making his collection. These shops will stand firmly behind their sales, giving the purchaser a guarantee that the object is what it is sold to be. There are also dealers who haven't so much knowledge but do have a knack for recognizing what is good—a talent for picking pieces with good lines or form—and then there are dealers who have neither knowledge nor knack but carry things they consider popular or faddish that will sell quickly. And finally there are shops whose owners are honest but do not have the knowledge and training necessary to classify them as experts. These shops carry desirable articles on the whole, but they also may have, unbeknownst to them, articles that are fakes, having acquired them with the understanding they were what they were represented to be. The trick is to have enough knowledge to recognize each type of shop for what it is and to know a fake when you see one, so that, unlike the lady in the story, your purchases will be exactly what you think they are.

Happily, all buyers of antique furniture are not attracted to the same things. There is the connoisseur whose hobby has turned into a passion. He is interested in pieces of the highest quality, and they are, naturally, in the highest price range. There are those who prefer reproductions—and no reason not to—but the lines should be good and correct and the piece should be priced as a copy and not as an antique. Whatever class of articles is acquired, be sure the price is right.

When you purchase a piece of furniture, whether fifty or two hundred years old, there are certain facts to keep in mind in determining the age, authenticity, and value of the article. The first impression of the piece must be good; otherwise dismiss it. Line, proportion, condition, and internal evidence of genuineness must always be seriously considered. Line and proportion are obvious at the first glance if the eye has been correctly trained; you will not have to check the internal evidence if line and proportion are not pleasing. Nor will you have to if the condition is poor. People often minimize the importance of condition. The average person is optimistic and will underestimate the extent and the cost of necessary repairs.

The following are ideas to keep in mind when you take this initial glance:

1. Are the lines good?
2. Compare remembered features of authenticated pieces seen in museums, books, and so on, with the item being examined.
3. Does it have artistic merit?
4. Was it well made to begin with?
5. Is it in good enough shape to be useful or will it have to be restored?

Furniture varies in condition, from the ideal "proof" to the most blatant fakes. To be proof, furniture must not have been refinished or have received any restoration. Restoration generally covers more tampering than repair. To restore means to bring back an object to its former state by the use of substitute parts. Repairs generally refer to small matters such as cleaning, reaffixing broken parts, regluing, and the like, without substituting new parts to any great extent.

There are various terms used to describe condition—re-creation, reconstruction, glorifying, converting, marriage, reproduction—all of which add up to the accusation of FAKE. A fake is made as an actual deception and is intended to be mistaken for what it is not. A reproduction honestly made as a reproduction, and sold by the maker as such, may become a fake when offered by an unscrupulous dealer as a true antique.

Another way in which dishonest dealers cheat their customers is by passing off nineteenth-century revival pieces as antiques. These had their origin in the popular revival following the Paris Exposition of 1867. At that time English cabinetmakers carefully constructed furniture, using the books and plans of Chippendale, Hepplewhite, and Sheraton. It is not always easy to distinguish the nineteenth-century copies from the period eighteenth-century articles. It is, however, gratifying to know there are dealers who will acknowledge them, as indicated by an advertisement I saw that read: "A beautiful find. Pair of Chippendale-style arm-chairs handsomely carved in rich brown mahogany. These chairs are in perfect condition and are unusually sturdy and comfortable. England circa 1860." Far better to call a spade a spade, and leave no doubt in the customer's mind. There is nothing wrong with these Centennial revival pieces; they were, on the whole, admirably made. What is wrong is when they are knowingly misrepresented as eighteenth century and priced accordingly.

The word "reconstruction" may cover anything from making furniture from old wood to expanding six original antique chairs to a set of twelve, which results in destroying the value of the six. "Glorifying" involves selecting a legit-imate article of antique furniture and adding devices, orna-mentation, or any desirable features that are not on the original, with the aim to increase the value. Some of the tricks of the glorifier are additions of inlay and carving to plain pieces, substituting parts from other pieces, and mis-mating. This last might include assembling fourposter beds from stray parts, cutting over tops or bases of highboys so they will match, equipping a simple secretary with an odd bookcase, or adding a piecrust edge to a pedestal table. "Marriage" describes the union of two unrelated pieces to produce another of higher value.

The term "converting" is sometimes used to cover several of the practices described above. A good craftsman is able to produce almost any article of furniture that is in demand and will bring a good price. Consider sofa tables: they are very rare and in great demand. Most of those seen in shops, if not entirely new, are made from old cheval-mirror supports. For the past number of years, owning a breakfront bookcase has become a status symbol. An expert craftsman will take a late-eighteenth-century wardrobe and replace the blind panels of the wooden doors with thirteen panes of glass each, replace the lower drawers with double doors, and add a wing to each side, thus producing a coveted and costly piece of furniture.

Since today the demand is for smaller articles of furniture, a very common form of converting is to reduce a large piece to a small one, both in length and depth. When drawers are present, this takes considerable skill. Converting on a large scale is usually directed toward desired pieces of the late eighteenth century, where the price difference between the mediocre and the desirable is considerable. Converting can be profitable.

Fraudulent additions and alterations are done with the aim of lifting a piece from a lower price range into a higher one. When this is successfully achieved, it must have been done by an experienced craftsman at a great cost of time and money. Consequently the article created will be in a price range that will attract only affluent collectors. Collecting or accumulating antiques advantageously requires knowledge and technical training that many people do not have the time or inclination to acquire. Thus, when you buy expensive antiques, it is advisable to acquire them from dealers who are willing to furnish a guarantee as to their true condition, and who will take them back if later they prove to be fakes. The alternative is to procure the services of an acceptable appraiser who can make a detailed examination of the article in question and, with the necessary experience and perception, evaluate the article *before it is purchased.*

If you are interested in buying less costly authentic antiques, you are not likely to run into the same problems. If changes or glorifications are made, they are done by an artisan with less skill than the craftsmen mentioned above, and are more easily detected. A concerned person can, with a little study, acquaint himself on how to recognize frauds. Not only will this added knowledge broaden his appreciation of antique furniture, but it may result in his acquiring an enviable collection of true antiques.

IX

Exterior Appearance

It is impossible to stress too much the importance of the initial glance when considering antique furniture, for that glance can prevent costly mistakes and wasted hours of examination. Unless you are in the trade, no piece should be contemplated whose size and style will not fit comfortably into your home. Often people purchase items because they are cheap, and their houses become increasingly crowded until there is scarcely room for the occupants; any charm the rooms might have had has vanished in the clutter. Ponder this first: if you cannot picture the article in a suitable position in your home, forget it. If you decide it is something that can be used advantageously, look further. Is it attractive aesthetically, something to be lived with happily? There are times and places that undesirable pieces have to be lived with, but this is not so when you are free to choose what to buy. O.K., it *is* a piece of furniture that you can live with happily and something that fits well in your home. Now are the lines and proportions correct; that is, are they jarring? Do they comply with the canons of good style and design? This is important. There may be some little thing jutting out at the wrong place, some incorrect addition. Think over pieces you have seen in museums and in antique-furniture books. Now how does it strike you? Going through these various items mentally may sound as though it will take a long time, but actually this first impression comes in a flash, an approach through the senses. If everything clicks in this first intuitive glance, then take a thorough look at the exterior of the article.

Condition

The condition of furniture is a factor in deciding whether or not it should be purchased. In Chapter VIII it was stated that most people underestimate the cost of repairs and restoration. Unless you are able to do them yourself, you should at the outset face squarely the extent of repairs necessary to put an article into usable condition. In England and America there is no set rule of how much repair may be made before an article is no longer considered an antique. Under French law an antique article offered for sale must be at least 90 percent original. In general, collectors do not consider a piece valuable if its replaced parts amount to more than 10 percent of the entire piece, or if its original shape or design has been altered. This is one of the times that common sense must act as a guide. It stands to reason that more restoration may be accepted in a rare piece than in an ordinary one. In the case of a Philadelphia Chippendale side chair, for instance, a buyer should be willing to overlook considerable damage. However, if it is a fairly common piece, such as a plain chest of drawers, which does not bring a large price even in good condition, there is a chance that the restoration will cost more than the chest is worth. If you are in doubt, you would be wise to call in a cabinetmaker and get an estimate of the cost of repairs.

Patina

Patina is an important sign of a genuine antique. Used in connection with antique furniture, patina is that mellowness and texture of surface color or condition attained by age as a result of long usage and repeated polishings. It is dirt that has sunk into the grain of the wood over the years as differences of temperature and humidity have caused it to open and shut. Dirt settles on the back and side edges that go against walls, and these edges eventually get quite dark. Wherever fingers touch, the moisture of the skin causes dust to stick, and this sinks into the grain even when the surface is polished. Age alone can produce this patina; once destroyed, it is impossible to replace. The patina of antique furniture should be guarded carefully so that the color of old wood shows use and not abuse. If the evidence of age and wear is removed, not only is charm lost but the value of the piece is vastly decreased. It is natural not to want deposits of grime and dust on a furniture surface, but with careful treatment these deposits, as well as paint, can be removed without damage. Unfortunately, there is now a much-used labor-saving process on the market in which an article is dipped into a stripping vat to remove offensive varnish or stain, and with it goes the original patina. This stripping liquid—as also occurs with paint or varnish remover used in too drastic applications—seeps into the wood and leaves the exterior of the piece looking dead, all life taken from it. This is something the buyer must beware of.

The color that finished wood takes on is caused not only by exposure to the air but also by the kind of polish used and how often it is applied. The tendency is for the shade to darken. But if the surface is in strong sunlight it will become bleached, changing slightly in mahogany from red to brown, and in walnut first to a golden shade and in time to a grayish color. The color will vary on different parts of the antique, since the sun does not shine on all surfaces to the same extent; thus a tabletop will often differ in color from the frieze and the legs.

Forgers and fakers find that patina is the most difficult thing to reproduce in a way to deceive anyone who has given it some study. They try to get around it by using old wood that has once served another purpose. But no amount of old wood is likely to contain two boards of matching color, and seldom will the wood be exactly the width, length, and thickness required. Somewhere it must have been cut, and the color of the cut will reveal the story.

When checking the patina on the exterior of an article of furniture, look at the out-of-sight parts as well as the surfaces in plain view. Check under chair arms and under the sides of tables where fingers grasp to lift or move the furniture, around the handles and knobs of case pieces where polishing over the years has left its impression, and on the front and sides of drawers, especially if they are large, because people have a tendency to open a drawer by the handles, but to push it back by holding the front edges and the front part of the sides.

Time gives the unfinished surfaces of the exterior, such as the backs of cabinet pieces, a mellowness. Time-aged and unvarnished mahogany is lighter and grayer than the varnished surfaces of the same wood. Old wood has a bloom, whereas new wood stained to simulate age has a dull, dirty look. Look under tabletops, under the arms and seats of chairs, on the back and side edges of pieces that have stood against the wall, on the hidden and unpolished surfaces of legs. When one's eyes become acquainted with the tint of old wood, any intrusion becomes obvious and the owner will be firm in not permitting a good antique to be drastically cleaned to such an extent that it loses the patina acquired over the years.

Signs of Use

Obviously, any article of furniture that has been in use for a century or more will show normal signs of that use. There is cause for suspicion when the signs are not present. This is not always so—there is furniture that has been protected and sheltered—but most antique furniture that has been around for one or two hundred years will show the effects of daily living and of cleaning. Evidence of natural wear is apparent in the dullness of sharp edges; tops may show stains from liquids, or marring from accidents, such as dishes that were too hot; legs may be dented and scratched, especially near the floor, as a result of having been hit by brooms or, in more recent times, by carpet sweepers and vacuum cleaners. The lower portion of chair legs may be worn down and polished from continual dragging of the chair into position over the years; this is especially so of the rear legs. Cross stretchers may show where heels have left their mark. In some cases wear has reached such an extent that legs or feet have been cut off and repaired or replaced. Some parts of Early American furniture, such as the turned button or knob feet of butterfly and tavern tables, may have been so worn down by decay, worms, or use that replacement was, and is, the only answer. This is justifiable, but since these tables are rare in their original condition, and command an enormous price on

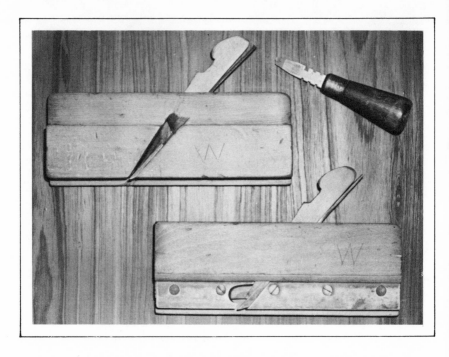

CARPENTER'S TOOLS, MADE BY AND BELONGING TO JOHN WILKENS,
SAVANNAH CABINETMAKER, CIRCA 1835.

ABOVE, LEFT: *a simple molding plane. Used for making
beads on plank or board corners.* RIGHT: *a steel
glass cutter or, when reversed, a small screwdriver.
Gauges at the sides are for chipping off edges of glass.*
BOTTOM: *a plow plane, for making grooves along the end of a board.*
OPPOSITE PAGE, TOP: *a jack plane. The largest hand-size plane
used for dressing down large boards. They come in various
sizes, the length varies from 12 to 17 inches.
The metal parts were made in Sheffield, England;
the wooden parts (of persimmon wood) by John Wilkens.*
CENTER: *a smoothing plane. Length 6 to 8 inches.
Used to make better-fitting edges on boards.*
BOTTOM: *a brace or bitstock. For boring holes. The center
is called an "elbow"; to the left is the "chuck," into which
the bit or drill is inserted; to the right is the "knob" or
"button." An attachment adjusts to different sizes
of bits and screwdrivers.*

today's market, a careful examination should be made. The replacements are generally smoother and more perfect than the rest of the table. With careful scrutiny, or with the blade of a pocketknife, a fine cut may be found between the base of the leg and the top of the new foot. The original table legs were turned from a single length of wood, and there was no cut or groove.

There are instances when legs of furniture have been cut down. A chair might have been lowered to make it more comfortable as a slipper chair. I saw this once on a fine American Sheraton-style chair that had been part of a set of eight dining chairs. Tables have been cut down for special purposes, or simply because the base of the legs or feet has worn away from use or dry rot and had to be cut off. To restore them to the proper height (in tables, usually twenty-seven to twenty-nine inches), additions are sometimes spliced on. A keen eye and a good pocket glass can detect the diagonal lines of such repairs. These are normal signs of wear and such corrections are acceptable. Just remember that when additions are present, a piece should not command the same price as it would if the object was in proof condition.

Tool Marks

The marks left by the tools of the early cabinetmakers on the exterior surfaces of antique furniture can be detected by touch and feel as well as by sight. A young lady took several chairs to a school for the blind to have new rush seats made to replace the worn ones. Among the new ones she had received as a wedding present ten years before were included two similar late-eighteenth-century chairs, which were signed. The blind man whom she had engaged immediately identified the two old ones. Although the blind have a keener sense of touch, it is possible for the sighted to feel the traces of the old tools. While you are looking at an object under consideration with a judicious eye, checking style, proportion, condition, patina, and general effect, it is almost instinctive to rub your hand over the top, back, sides, and raw edges. What is it that you are looking for? Across the top of even the most faultlessly finished article a slight undulation, a wavy sensation, can be detected. This is even more pronounced on drawer bottoms, under tabletops, on the backs of chests, cupboards, and cabinets, and also on the interiors of doors, where these marks are obvious to the eye. In the past when a piece of furniture was made, the lumber was first hand-sawed; then the wood was dressed with a heavy jack plane that had a slightly curved cutting edge to the blade, nearly three inches wide, and left a wavy appearance on the surface. Usually the craftsmen, being practical people, did not go further in finishing the parts that did not show—consequently the ridges and hollows.

On the edges of the backboards of corner cupboards, desks, chests of drawers, and so on, the marks that are felt and seen are from the ripsaws used for coarse work. These saws, worked vertically either by water power or by two men, left parallel straight scratches very different from the curved mark of the modern buzz saw.

Inlay

Be sure to examine carefully the exterior of antique furniture that is enhanced by inlay; its presence may indicate that unscrupulous persons have attempted to raise the value of an article. Inlaid pieces are considered more decorative than others and hence are more in demand. Since decorative inlay was a feature of eighteenth- and some early-nineteenth-century furniture, the easiest fakes to spot contain such glaring inconsistencies as a satinwood shell or sunburst on an Empire or Victorian piece. A large mahogany sleigh-front chest of drawers with an inlaid addition to spruce it up cries out that it is wrong. Detection is more difficult when inlay is added to the plain surface of a piece made during the period when inlay was used. Woodworking specialty houses in large cities offer a selection of standard prefabricated borders and medallions, including the eagle and cockleshell. Modern factory-made inlays are crude compared to the antique ones; the contrast is obvious when the two are placed side by side. When a plain surface is inlaid, it has to be scraped down about a sixteenth of an inch; thus the old patina and polish are destroyed and the grain is left as open as when the timber was first planed. To close it as it was before would take a couple of centuries, and that scraped surface gives it away. After all these years real eighteenth-century inlay will be found forced up in places, because the main timber has shrunk. If inlaid lines are countersunk, or everywhere level with the surface, they are apt to be recent additions.

Carving

In spite of the commonly held opinion that there are no wood-carvers today who can match the skill of the old masters, any skilled contemporary craftsman who wishes to take the time to work up his detail can do a job that will compare favorably with the early carvers. Nevertheless, whether the carving is of a patera or on legs, backs, arms, and so on, it is possible to ascertain when it was done. Carving on old furniture is always above the surface of the rest of the timber and always very bold. The eighteenth-century cabinetmaker did not have to economize with his timber; he cut away and down into the wood he was carving, leaving the design standing up crisply on its own. Flat or countersunk carving must have been added at a later date. The good carving on old chairs and settees is so sharp that it is possible to cut your hand while feeling and rubbing it.

Many pieces that were worthy in their original state have been carved at a later date, losing their value in the process. This is particularly true of simple Chippendale chairs, but the added carving is inevitably flat or countersunk and easy to detect. During the Victorian period, cabinetmakers and factories made countless new "Chippendale" chairs; the chairs were carved with larger chisels than those of the eighteenth century and they left different marks. Victorian workmen also economized on wood, resulting in carving that is much flatter.

Style

After you have checked the general condition of the piece and noted some of its finer details, it is time to make a fuller determination of style than a first glance can provide. Bear in mind what you have learned earlier in this book, in other informative books and pictures on antique furniture, and in the study of furniture in museums about the important features of different styles. Always remember that the article of furniture being examined could not have been made until the style proclaimed was in vogue. Whether it was made at that time or later can be ascertained only by a thorough examination of the exterior and interior of the article. Some of the exterior elements to check have just been given, and consideration of interior evidence will be found in the following chapter. What is necessary now is to take a closer look at various exterior structural parts to see whether there are false aspects to a piece of furniture that will justify thinking that it was made later than the predominant style features might indicate, or whether it has been added to, converted, or assembled. This closer look should include such components as the apron, drawer moldings, double-section pieces, doors, tripods of pedestal tables, proportion, overhang of tops of pieces, and hardware, including pulls and escutcheons.

Proportion

It is probably the proportion or lack of proportion that will strike you first. Your eye will no doubt recognize when the proportions are wrong; if not, a tape measure will confirm it. The eighteenth- and early-nineteenth-century cabinet-makers were artists, and it can be accurately stated that nothing they constructed was out of proportion. If a piece is old and not in proportion, it is not worthy and should not be considered. There are certain basic measurements to keep in mind. The height of a bookcase was always greater than the width. Kneehole desks or writing tables in English pieces were usually five feet wide by three feet nine inches deep, and the height from the floor to the top of space for the knees was two feet. Dining tables were usually two feet four inches high. There are exceptions to these rules in pieces that were especially made for a particular person, but the proportions remain the same. If a piece looks to be in the right proportion, and all the details are correct, it is probably genuine even if it is unusually large. If a piece looks wrong, check it carefully; the unusually small chest and the exceptionally slender bookcase are open to suspicion.

Aprons, Pedestal Tables, Overhang

The apron in tables is the piece connecting the legs, just under the top; in chairs, it is beneath the seat; in cabinets, chests of drawers, and such, it is along the base. The apron is also referred to as the skirt. When you find an apron around the underside of a circular tabletop, you can be assured the table is of Victorian vintage. These aprons were screwed onto the top, and sometimes have been removed to give the table an earlier appearance. If this is so, it can be discovered by checking for screw holes at intervals around the underside of the table; in some cases they have been plugged. In the case of aprons of chairs and wall furniture, you must depend on tool marks to judge the age.

When you look at a pedestal table, be sure to check whether or not it has a platform base. This will tell you that it is not of eighteenth-century origin but dates sometime after 1835, since the platform base was popular during the Victorian period. A pedestal dining table, which is usually rectangular or oval, can have two pedestals and one leaf, three pedestals and two leaves, four pedestals and three leaves, or five pedestals and four leaves. A table should be at least four feet across, and some are as wide as six feet. The average two-pedestal table is about four feet six inches wide, nine feet long with the leaf, and twenty-eight inches high. Beware of inlaid pedestal dining tables, because the period ones were always perfectly plain. Four legs on each pedestal are considered earlier and better than three. If the edge of the top is plain, the legs should be plain; if the edge is reeded, the legs should be reeded. Does the pedestal have rings? If so, it is of a later date: the more rings, the later the date. Note these items carefully, since pedestals and tops are often mismated, an old top on a new base, or the reverse.

Look at the overhang of all tabletops. If it is more than an inch on either side, the chances are that the top does not belong to the base. All pieces made to stand against the wall should have an overhang at the back of at least two inches to allow for the skirting board.

Drawers

Drawers of the better pieces made in the Queen Anne or Chippendale style usually have what is called "a lipped molding" around the edge. This means the edge of the drawer extends in a lip form to overlap the edge of the drawer opening. The drawers of the better pieces of the Hepplewhite and Sheraton periods have what is termed "a cock-beaded edge," a narrow raised molding around the edge of the drawer. When this is found on chest or desk drawers, it is safe to assume the article was made after 1775 or 1780. Cock-beading was always glued. When it is pinned, usually in three places, consider the piece clumsily repaired, or made during the Victorian period or later.

Double-Section Pieces and Doors

Furniture of double heights, such as secretaries, bookcases, chests on chests, and so forth, will be found with both sections made from the same piece of timber, the top and bottom always of the same thickness. Also the stiles of the doors should be the same width in both the top and the bottom sections. Notice the door or doors. Single doors always open to the right; the lock or handle is on the left and the hinges on the right. They were never made with a left-handed person in mind. When double doors are found, there are three hinges on each door, and they are not seen from

Side chair, often called a "Baltimore chair,"
American, 1815 to 1820. Painted dark blue,
with a gilded and stenciled design, lyre-shaped splat.

*Split-banister-back armchair, American,
made in New England circa 1710. Maple.*

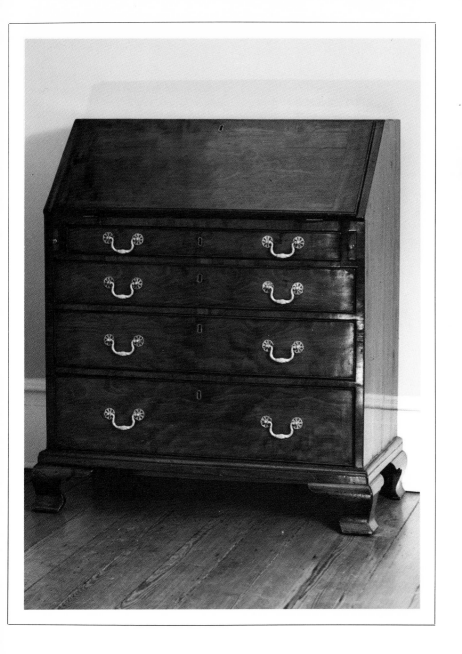

Chippendale-style slant-top desk, English, circa 1770.
Mahogany, with bail handles and ogee bracket feet.

Empire-style pier table, American, circa 1818.
Painted to simulate rosewood, with gold-stenciled design
resembling brass inlay. White marble top and ionic columns, claw feet.
Sheraton-style mirror, American, circa 1810.
Gilded wood frame, with églomisé panel at top.

Sheraton-style chest of drawers, American, circa 1810.
Mahogany, swell front, turreted columns,
cock-beaded-edge drawers with rosette brasses.

Empire-style sugar chest, American, circa 1830.
Cherry and maple, with spool-turned legs.
Queen Anne–style lowboy, American, circa 1750.
Curly maple, lipped-edge drawers with batwing brasses,
cabriole legs with raised pad feet.

Hepplewhite-style demilune card table, American, circa 1790.
Mahogany, with holly string and sunburst inlay;
tapering legs with block feet.
Queen Anne–style card table, American, circa 1760.
Blocked front, restrained cabriole legs with raised pad feet.

Federal-style chair, American, circa 1815.
Curly maple, cane seat, acanthus-carved slat, curule legs.

the front, with the exception of corner cupboards, bedside commodes, and grandfather clocks. On the other pieces, the doors were hinged into the face of the side timbers, so that just the knuckle of the hinge can be seen and then only when you look at it from the side. Where the two doors meet, a narrow, thin astragal molding of wood or brass was screwed on, not pinned. In the Victorian period the moldings became much wider.

Furniture Mounts

There are several things to watch for. As you become accustomed to the look of authentic pieces, such variances as a Hepplewhite-style top sitting on a Chippendale base, a newly carved piecrust edge added to the plain top of a pedestal table, inlay inserted in the mahogany veneer of an Empire sideboard, or drop leaves added to a simple one-drawer table will be spotted at the first glance. In conjunction with this, you should also be familiar with the styles of furniture hardware and handles. It is just as disturbing to find Chippendale batwing brasses on the drawers of an ogee-front Empire sideboard, or pressed-glass pulls on a Queen Anne maple highboy. Usually this particular kind of exchange was done not to defraud but to imitate the latest fashion or to "beautify" the article. I prefer the term "furniture mounts" instead of the more usual "brasses" in referring to these pulls, handles, and escutcheons, since they were made of wood, brass, Sheffield plate, ivory, pressed glass, and even porcelain—from the late-eighteenth-century decorative ones made of Battersea enamel to the Victorian knobs of plain white porcelain.

It increases the value of an article enormously if it has retained its original mounts; also they are a big help in dating the object. However, if they have been lost during the

years—all or only two or three—and if it is a good piece in
other respects, replacement is definitely worth considering.
The important thing is that the replacements should be of the
same period as the piece and conform in every way. It is
almost impossible to distinguish original brass mounts from
good reproductions. There are companies reproducing by
hand excellent copies of old hardware out of fine materials.
Often it is possible to tell if the original brasses have been
replaced by looking on the inside of the drawer front to
check the old post holes; they may have been plugged up and
new holes made. Remember it is possible to get brasses of the
same size, and the new posts can be put in the old post holes.
However, the threaded posts that came into use about 1700
continued to be crudely made well into the nineteenth century, and the machine or die-cut screw thread used in
modern hardware can be distinguished with the use of a
magnifying glass if one is in the least observant. An important fact to keep in mind is that many English and American
antiques with drawers had wooden pulls. Unfortunately it
has been the opinion of far too many people that the piece
would be more decorative or bring a higher price if the original wooden knobs—mahogany, in many cases—were replaced by brasses. It usually would have been better to leave
the piece with its original knobs and not attempt to dress it
up. The interior of the piece reveals what has happened,
since the single plugged hole is most visible. Check and be
sure that the handles of all drawers are in line; if not, the
piece has been tampered with.

Escutcheons

An escutcheon in connection with brass handles is a
plate having a keyhole; the plate is placed over a hole cut in

the wood to receive the key of a lock. The escutcheons used on each part of the furniture were originally identical in size, shape, and design; if the drawers and doors are in line, the escutcheons should be in line, too. They were always placed in the center of the drawer or of the stile of the door, halfway between top and bottom. If they are not in this position, there is cause for doubt; the piece may have been meddled with. Genuine eighteenth-century escutcheons are rounded at the bottom. Those with square bottoms are of the period from about 1835 on. The majority of eighteenth-century furniture had escutcheons. When there are no escutcheons, the piece is under suspicion. Escutcheons are also found surrounded by an attached plate, of batwing design in the Queen Anne and Chippendale periods, and square or oval in the classic or Federal period. Ivory escutcheons were at first used on small articles such as tea caddies; in the late eighteenth and early nineteenth centuries they were used on cabinetwork.

Brasses

The Early American furniture craftsmen went to their local blacksmiths for wrought-iron hinges, nails, screws, and simpler locks, but they ordered brasses from England for their fine well-constructed furniture. There was practically no craft of this sort in America until Paul Revere gave up silversmithing for copper and its alloys. And the brass founders of England made a superior product. Actually, as was true with other products, the English Parliament was prone to protect home industries at the expense of the Colonies. Colonial brass founding had been forbidden by the lawmakers of England, and English producers of furniture brass sought American trade before, and even after, the

American Revolution. They published detailed catalogues depicting their wares in copperplate engravings, showing handles, finials, hinges, escutcheons, and the like, each with an identifying number. These were published throughout the eighteenth and nineteenth centuries, with no descriptive text or prices quoted, giving the American cabinetmaker a free hand to show them to the customer for decisions without disclosing any secrets or prices. It is interesting to note that they continued to carry brasses appropriate for styles that had long since gone out of fashion, an advantage to anyone who wished to replace a broken or lost brass of an older style. These brass-makers catered to the desires of the new republic in the same way the pottery- and china-makers did. Brasses that carried a stamped relief such as the coat of arms of an eagle with shield and stars, the eagle's claws grasping the arrows of war and the olive branch of peace, were regularly advertised.

Hardware Styles

Each period had its fashion in furniture mounts. The hardware a piece of furniture exhibits can be an asset in identifying its style, although, as has been previously stated, this alone cannot be accepted in judging age but must be taken in conjunction with other clues that are present. As in other stylistic structures, one period's fashions overlapped another's. Refer to the sketches accompanying the written descriptions on the following pages to get an accurate picture of the various styles.

The Queen Anne style, beginning in the eighteenth century, continued to use brasses that were popular during the preceding William and Mary period: drop handles, teardrop or pear drop, the name indicating their form to some extent.

They were attached to a brass plate behind the handles, and the plates were generally ornamented with designs. The drop handle was attached to the drawer by a wire pin, called a cotter pin, bent and driven into the wood, making a not very strong connection. A later form was the bail handle, which is somewhat in the shape of a half circle; these were more often used with a brass backplate roughly in the shape of a bat's wing—termed the batwing plate—that was either plain or chased. On the lacquered furniture of the William and Mary period, elaborate pierced and chased mounts were found that had escutcheons and key plates embellished with cherubs and other ornate designs. The simpler Queen Anne taste did not accept these fancy forms, and replaced them with plainer brasswork. Handles were usually of the bail pattern and attached to unadorned or slightly chased batwing—sometimes called willow-pattern—plates. These were cut out by hand or were cast in a mold, and the edges were generally beveled. The bails were held in place by bolts, or posts, threaded like a screw, extending through the front of the drawer and fastened on the inside with nuts. Matching escutcheons were often used. Early-eighteenth-century furniture in America had these same types of brasses; indeed, as mentioned above, they were ordered from England.

During the Chippendale period, there was a popular theory that brass mounts lent a decorative quality to the general appearance of the furniture to which they were attached. On the ordinary or less expensive pieces, the handles and escutcheons and key plates continued to be the plain types that had been used for some years. They were pierced or fretted, or altogether plain. With the more elaborate furniture, especially the French-influenced pieces, the handles, escutcheons, and key plates were in the most enriched rococo manner, comparing favorably with the intricate ormolu mounts on contemporary French furniture. In some

QUEEN ANNE   CHIPPENDALE

batwing brass with bail handle   *pierced batwing brass with bail handle*

CHIPPENDALE      *bail handle*

instances fretwork mounts of brass were used purely for purposes of decoration, quite apart from their use as handles, key plates, and escutcheons. The custom of enhancing grand, sophisticated chests of drawers, highboys, lowboys, and case furniture with impressive brasses was practiced by cabinetmakers working in the Chippendale style in America as well, particularly in such centers as Massachusetts, Rhode Island, New York, Philadelphia, and Charleston.

The furniture mounts used in the classic-revival style of the Adam brothers, Hepplewhite, and Sheraton show the lightness, as well as the other physical traits, that identify this period. On Adam-designed furniture the brasses have the same characteristic delicacy and care that mark all their work, both architecturally and decoratively. The patterns vary to a large extent with the individual pieces, but all convey a sense of beauty and refinement. Hepplewhite, who captured the Adam lightness of line, used handles of the bail type, but unlike the earlier Chippendale ones, they were attached to brass backplates that were predominantly oval, oblong, octagonal, or round. Key plates were small and usually consisted of ivory or brass set flush with the woodwork. The plates of thin brass that began to be used about 1779 were not cast or made by hand but were stamped from dies in three-dimensional relief, which produced impressions of

oval escutcheons with bail handles

SHERATON *knob handle*

ornamental designs of classic scenes, cornucopias, acorns, oak leaves, flowers, grapes, animals, and so forth. In the new republic, cabinetmakers were using brasses stamped with patriotic themes such as the popular eagle and stars. Along with brass, Sheffield-plate and enameled backplates were occasionally used, as well as ivory and inlaid escutcheons.

The same handles continued to be used for some years in the Sheraton period, but new styles also appeared. One was a round or oval ornamental plate with a round or oval knob handle attached to the top. Another was a round bail suspended from the mouth of a lion, referred to as a lion-and-ring handle, which was first used in England about 1795. And still another was an octagonal-shaped plate with a bail of the same shape. Often the furniture was fitted with brass or wooden knobs instead of bail handles.

On the furniture called Regency in England and Federal in America, these Sheraton-style brasses remained in use. Brass knobs projecting about an inch from the surface and an inch and a half in diameter were popular from about 1815 to 1830. Phyfe used them on his tables and sewing stands in the Sheraton manner. In America, these were often ornamented with patriotic symbols such as the eagle or the head of George Washington.

Glass knobs came into fashion about 1815 and lasted

until about 1840, varying greatly in quality. They are found chiefly on heavy bureaus and sideboards in the Empire style. They were made in great numbers and in many colors at several glass factories throughout the United States, but most were made of clear glass, or opal or white. They were attached by screws or metal rods. The knobs were frequently broken or lost, and it is almost impossible to find duplicates. Knobs of cut glass are of better workmanship than the others and hence much more desirable. About 1810, mahogany knobs held in place by wood screws were current. As was stated earlier, collectors or dealers often replace these knobs with brasses. This is unfortunate, for they were meant to harmonize with the overall effect of rich dark wood and not to break the surface, as the bright brass mounts do.

I would like to emphasize again the importance placed by collectors on the presence of the original mounts. They add greatly to the value of the piece; they were always kept lacquered and in brilliant appearance by continual polishings, as they should be today. It is documented that on many of the Southern plantations there was one slave whose single duty was to keep the brasses polished, so as to achieve the look sought by the original cabinetmaker.

Locks

While writing about brasses, let me add a word about locks, although they cannot be observed by looking at the exterior of a piece. Eighteenth-century locks or door bolts are never stamped with a name or patent number; this practice came in with the second quarter of the nineteenth century. These later locks may have been made by Bramah, Barron, Chubb, or some other lock patentee, in which case they may be stamped with a crown, the initial of the reigning monarch (GR, WR, or VR), and the maker's name, with the word "PATENT" in capitals. Occasionally the maker's name was omitted; Early Victorian locks, for example, are often stamped with the crown and cypher, and the words "Patent Secure Lever Lock," or something similar, but no name. Sometimes the marks of a file are discernible on one side of the levers; these marks show that the name or patent number has been destroyed to imply that the article of furniture was made earlier. With the old eighteenth-century locks and door bolts the cases are of brass, but the actual levers and bolts are of steel and are either square or oblong. Victorian bolts have a circular shaft and button-type escutcheons. These were made in large quantities in 1846 and remained popular for a long time. The fixing of locks should be noted, the point being that a Continental lock was generally let into a slot in the front of the drawer, whereas the usual English practice was to cut a place for the lock so that the back of it lay flush with the back of the drawer front.

X

A Look at the Interior

Open the doors, pull out the drawers, turn the piece over if necessary, but make a thorough search of the interior. This final observation will conclude your tests of the authenticity of the furniture being examined. Most people shopping for antique furniture feel reluctant to ask the dealer or salesman to move a piece in question out from the wall into a better light, or to turn it over so that they may see it more clearly. You should feel no hesitancy in making such a request; it is to the advantage of both buyer and dealer that the customer be completely satisfied. If, after the purchase, an article is found by an authority to be not what is claimed, a respectable dealer will have to make amends or be confronted by a dissatisfied customer whose talk will cost him trade in the future. And it is a shock to the buyer when he finds he has paid several hundred or even several thousand dollars for a secretary, sideboard, or whatever that is either a fake or has been altered beyond a state meriting the title "antique." This can all be avoided by being firm at the beginning and asking the dealer if you may examine the article thoroughly.

Although you have learned a lot by checking the exterior, there is more to consider on the interior. Many dealers, as well as buyers, fail to do this. They find a piece that appears to be good, and reasonably priced, but are afraid to take the time to look further for fear it will get away from them. They take a chance and too often regret later that they were not more cautious.

Secondary Woods

Assume that you are in a shop looking at a secretary-bookcase priced at $2,400—not a purchase to enter into casually. Many of the items checked on the exterior must be checked again on the interior. The condition is still of prime consideration: if the article is in too bad shape to be used, it is of no value and should be dismissed from your mind. From the exterior examination you have decided that the outer physical condition is satisfactory: the wood is mahogany with a line inlay of satinwood; it is in the Hepplewhite style; the brasses are in the correct fashion but not original; the top and base are compatible; the splay feet have had some restoration (as is often necessary, owing to the feet receiving too much weight from loaded drawers); and the glazed doors are fixed with glass panes set into a woodwork lattice pattern of straight astragal bars instead of one sheet of glass with added fake astragal bars. Where do you look now? Usually it comes naturally to pull out the drawers in the lower section, one at a time. Look first to see what the secondary wood is. Secondary woods are those which do not show on a piece of furniture, such as the structural pieces used for internal bracing, or for backboards and shelving, and those on which mahogany and other woods are glued. They are the woods used for the bottoms and sides of the drawers, and it is possible to determine from them whether the piece was made in England or America. When oak is found on the interior of drawers, you can be almost sure the piece is of English origin. But not so with pine, since the English deal, or pine, is similar to that found in America. The drawers of Scottish pieces are apt to be of Scottish pine. This can be confusing because the grain is very similar to the Southern pine of the United States, which includes longleaf (*Pinus palustris*), slash pine (*Pinus elliotti*), and loblolly (*Pinus taeda*). However, Southern pine is a hardwood and Scottish pine is soft, which makes it possible to tell the difference.

Drawers

Careful observation must be given to the construction of the drawers. This is helpful in dating the piece as well as ascertaining that it has not been altered in any way. Drawer construction changed as time progressed. Drawers of the latter part of the seventeenth century and the early eighteenth century were rabbeted and nailed. They usually move on runners that fit into a groove about halfway up the side of the drawers. A broad dovetail sometimes shows at the front. This was followed by using the bottom boards of drawers to run on, fitting in a groove that went around the front and sides of the drawers. One or two nails in the back kept the drawer from rattling around. Where the bottom was very thick, it was chamfered to a quarter of an inch to fit into the

groove. These drawers had three or four stubby dovetails.
Up to 1770 the grain in the bottom boards of drawers ran
from front to back; after that the grain ran from side to side.
To allow for shrinkage, the eighteenth-century cabinetmaker
made the drawer bottoms in two or three pieces. In authentic
period drawers, the bottom and back boards are apt to be
split in places where the timber has shrunk. Continuing into
the latter part of the eighteenth century, drawer sides were
made lower than the bottom board and used as drawer runners. The dovetailing became finer, especially on the more
elegant furniture. Strips of wood found glued to the base of
the drawer as reinforcement to the runners denote modern
construction; when they are found on a piece stated to be
eighteenth century or a few years later, it is a giveaway. The
two sides of the drawer must be of the same timber, and the
dovetails must be the same, too. Any difference indicates the
piece has been restored, converted, or interfered with. All
drawers, large or small, should have a scribe mark to show
where the dovetail ends. If a drawer has been reduced in
depth, the scribe marks may have been cut through, the required amount taken off the sides and bottom board, and the
two parts flimsily joined together again. If, when you pull
out a drawer, you find it is "front-heavy"—that is, inclined
to fall out because of its own weight—you will know that the
drawer was originally much bigger and has a heavier front
than that needed for a drawer with the present dimensions.
In old furniture, regardless of size, the drawer never ran the
full depth of the piece; a gap of up to two inches was always
left between the drawer and the back of the piece to allow air
to circulate. On all good-quality English pieces the drawer
sides are of oak, with the top edges of the sides rounded. The
thinner the sides, the better the piece. If possible, while the
drawers are out, turn the piece upside down. You should find
that there are paler patches on the underside of the top,

corresponding to the drawers. When two drawers are side by side, they should be the same size. The runners on the interior drawer frame are usually worn down from the constant pulling back and forth of heavily laden drawers, and in many instances they have been replaced. This is an acceptable replacement, as the reason for it is understandable —the drawers would not otherwise be usable.

Dust Boards

Dust boards are boards placed between each drawer, completely separating them. As the term suggests, they prevent the dust from seeping through. Practically every English piece is supplied with dust boards, but they were seldom used on American pieces. Checking for these can be a further aid in placing the origin of an article such as the secretary-bookcase.

Undersurfaces

The undersides, backs, and interiors of old furniture were always left raw. Dust and time have given them a patination that speaks for itself. When stain, varnish, or shellac are on the undersurfaces of a piece, there is cause to doubt its authenticity. It could be either a reproduction or a reconstruction.

Tool Marks

The tactile evidence of tool marks was explained in the previous chapter, and the interior should be checked for them as well. Feel the underside of the top, under drawer bottoms, and along the interior of the sides for the undulating patterns left by the jack plane. They should be much more distinct than those on the exterior surfaces, which may have been finished more thoroughly and be smoother than the interior, although still covered with slight ridges and hollows. In addition, the exterior marks have been filled over the years with wax or finish, and are therefore not so obvious.

Scratches or marks produced by the scribing awl and the chisel should be apparent where corners are dovetailed together, and signs of the chisel will be seen in various places on the interior of pieces. The irregular chisel-cutting marks are easy to spot on the frames of tables, of desks, and on shaped bracket feet, as well as on various parts of sofas. The half-round gouging chisel was used to cut channels for screws. A flat chisel about a half-inch wide was used to mark the various parts of dismantled pieces for easy identification. The chisel was driven into the wood about a sixteenth of an inch: a single vertical cut made a straight line for the one; two in a V shape formed the five; and so on. These should have the slight unevenness characteristic of all handwork. When the piece has numbered parts showing they were done by the same chisel, you can be assured that they began life together and that the entire article with consistent idiosyncrasies was constructed by one cabinetmaker. Bedposts and sides were so numbered, as were both frames and slip seats of chairs. These marks can be a big help in telling if a set of chairs was made at one time or at different times. The marks are occasionally found on the drawer openings and drawers of chests of drawers, chests on chests, and highboys to facilitate replacing a drawer in the correct opening. Again, these marks will prove if a piece of furniture is all original or if it has been assembled.

Hardware—Nails

Familiarity with the use of nails, screws, wooden pins or dowels, and casters is a further help in checking the age of furniture. It is surprising how many people continue to accept the fallacy that if any parts of an article of furniture are nailed together it cannot be an antique. They believe that if furniture is old it must be pegged together, that nails are a comparatively modern invention. Iron nails go back to the Roman occupation of Britain; large numbers have been found there wrought by the Romans. These ancient nails have a striking resemblance to the type manufactured at the present time. The forging of nails was an industry of some importance in Great Britain up to the end of the seventeenth century, and only gave way to the advent of machine-headed nails. In America the earliest nails were imported from England, but the equipment needed to make nails was simple and the industry soon became widespread in the Colonies, where, as early as 1731, a nail factory is recorded. These so-called factory-made nails were hand-forged from iron bars that were probably imported from Russia or Sweden via England.

The material of the early nails was of high purity, soft, easily bent, but exceedingly tough and highly rust-resistant. Nails have been removed from furniture two hundred years old with the blue scale entirely intact and as bright as the day they were made. The early nails were of various patterns and sizes. On the whole, they were sharply rectangular in cross section and sharply pointed at the tip. The heads were usually squarish; those with larger heads were used most frequently for hinges. There was a small-headed nail that was employed for finishing in all phases of cabinetwork. Machinery for cutting nails was introduced in America about 1790. These cut nails were not quite as good as the hand-forged ones but cost much less. They were made of the same iron, although they were not as tough. Their points were square, because for some reason the machine was not able to make sharp points until much later. There is a resemblance between the hand-forged nails and the cut ones, but with careful examination the difference will be noticeable. The cut nails are thicker and less tapered and have an angular tip much different from the thin swordlike point of the hand-forged nail. Further, they show no hammer marks but have slight burrs along two opposite edges, made by the cutter. As with any handmade product, there is a difference in each hand-forged nail produced, whereas cut nails come out almost identical.

It is true that nails can help in setting a date on a piece of furniture; if a piece is put together entirely with hand-forged nails, it can be presumed to have been constructed prior to 1790 or 1800. A piece with cut nails must date in the nineteenth century. Unfortunately we cannot always rely on this method, since hand-forged nails continued to be made as late as 1877 in Philadelphia, as well as at village smithies on order from local carpenters, who didn't like the brittle and easily broken machine-made nails. Another thing to remember is that someone intent on producing a fake will remove hand-forged nails from old house timber and use them in his reconstructed furniture. Everything must add up: you cannot judge from one point, but must consider all factors before reaching a decision about the age and authenticity of any piece of furniture.

Dowels

Anyone familiar with woodworking knows that nails are used for one thing, and wooden pins or dowels (also called pegs) are used for another. When dowels were first used in making furniture is not known. They are found in primitive American furniture and in furniture from the entire eighteenth and nineteenth centuries. Old dowels were roughly polygonal and slightly tapered toward the point, made of the tougher hardwoods—birch, oak, hickory, maple, cherry, beech, and walnut. When a tabletop is made of several boards, they are doweled and glued together, edge to edge, to appear as a single board. The upper frames and stretchers of tables are usually doweled into the legs. Arms of chairs and seat members are frequently doweled together. Spare leaves of extension dining tables are doweled to make them match and fit together; the pins are glued into the holes on one board only. When a pin is driven into a round hole of proper size, it bites into the wood and sets firmly. In early furniture, even when the pins were cut off flush right after they were driven in, they slowly began to work their way out; the wood where the pins were driven shrank with time, but the pins remained the same in length, because hardwood does not shrink along the fiber. They will be found to project a sixteenth of an inch or more above the surface. This is a detail difficult to fake. Modern pins, which are cylindrical pieces of hardwood, are driven into kiln-dried wood, and when cut off flush they remain flush. The old dowels, made with plane, drawknife, and jackknife, were never exactly round or alike. Modern dowels come from a machine and are mathematically circular. They may be purchased from hardware stores or lumberyards. They ordinarily come in three-foot lengths and are an eighth of an inch to an inch in diameter. They are then cut to the required length. When perfectly round dowel ends are found in a piece of furniture, it has been taken apart and new dowels used in reassembling, or it is newly made.

Screws

Screws have been used in cabinetwork for several centuries, not as a replacement for nails or dowels but as a superior means of holding, such as in hinges for drop-leaf tables and cabinet doors. How far back they were in use is unknown, but Ramelli, an Italian engineer, mentions screws in his *Machine Book*, published in the sixteenth century. An Englishman named Moxon also mentioned them in a published work in 1678. To what extent they were used in these early times is uncertain. They were employed to fasten locks to doors in England. And by the 1750s they were finding favor in America among joiners, having been introduced into the Colonies during the early years of the eighteenth century. Screws can furnish important information in authenticating an article of furniture. Here is another way to test the cooperation of the seller: an ethical dealer should not mind having a prospective buyer remove a single screw, say, from a highly priced corner cupboard. The buyer may then be able to determine the approximate date of the article. Early screws had a flat surface at the end, which necessitated using a gimlet to drill a starting hole; for this reason, they can be very difficult to remove. Like the hand-forged nails, they were not uniform in length, and it is possible to find that every screw removed from the hinges of an eighteenth-century cupboard is of a different length. These early hand-made blunt-end screws were very expensive, and were treasured by the poorer provincial cabinetmakers, who could not afford to use them often. The prosperous urban cabinetmakers employed by the wealthy used them to a greater extent. Around 1815 machine-cut screws made their appearance, manufactured still with blunt ends. Since they were much cheaper, the handmade ones soon disappeared. The first pointed screw was made in England and shown at the 1851 Exhibition. They were not mass-produced until a few years later. A defrauder may cut the point off a machine-made screw to make the piece appear to be pre-1851, but a mass-produced screw cannot be made to look like the handmade article. The handmade blunt-end screws were seldom perfectly round; the screwdriver slot was shallow, narrow, and usually slightly or completely off center. Observed through a magnifying glass, the threads or spirals will show file marks. The early ones were quite crude. The machine-cut screws made after 1815, still with flat ends, were made uniformly and were cleanly cut; their heads were round and the driver slot was of uniform depth and centered. It is important to be able to distinguish between the hand-made and the machine-cut screws, since, for instance, a cup-board declared to be eighteenth century could not possibly have machine-made blunt-end screws. If screws were used to fasten the back of one part of a double-height piece, they should also have been used to fasten the back of the other part. If they were not, it is probably a married piece. About 1870 many cabinetmakers dipped their screws in glue before inserting them. If you experience difficulty in removing a screw, heat the tip of your screwdriver and let it rest on the head for a few seconds. If that does the trick, it probably reveals that the article was made after 1870.

Casters

Rightly, casters, also called rollers, should have been included in the preceding chapter, since they are an exterior appendage. But it seems more fitting to include them here with the other hardware. Casters are small wheels fitted with swivels, usually attached to the feet of furniture too heavy to lift easily but requiring frequent moving, such as armchairs, settees, and, occasionally, chests of drawers. This is another instance where some people incorrectly consider a type of hardware a fairly new invention: they look askance at a piece of furniture bearing casters. On the contrary, as early as 1700 in England furniture was made with casters, and soon afterward in America. It is rare, though, to find furniture fitted with its original casters. The early ones were made of two or three pieces of leather attached to swivels and the hub fitted up into the leg. The bucket caster of metal, usually brass, was introduced about 1760, and is seen on Chippendale-style pieces. Bucket casters of this type are manufactured today for reproduction furniture and to replace lost casters. The percentage of copper in the brass made today is not as high as it was in the eighteenth century and does not have the same green shade. The square box caster, also of brass, was used on a square leg and is generally found on pieces made between 1760 and 1800. Casters continued to be used on furniture, and about the third quarter of the nineteenth century, they began to appear in white porcelain as well, a definite sign of Victorian origin.

Don't be discouraged by the many abovementioned items to check. It is surprising how quickly you will be able to tell at a glance if something about the piece you are examining is not right. In that case, and if the price is high, it is wiser to disregard it. On the other hand, if it is reasonably priced and something you have been looking for over a long period to fit a certain space in your home, then check further. The important thing is to be aware of what you are buying and not pay more than the article is worth.

XI

Case Histories

There are various ways to acquire antique furniture. By the fortunate ones it is inherited, but by the majority of people it has to be acquired by purchase, and this brings up the question of where to find the antiques you are seeking. The ideal place is the shop of a well-recognized, knowledgeable, and trustworthy dealer, who not only stands behind what he is selling but will also instruct you in the fine points of the articles you want. Understandably, prices at such shops are usually higher than at others. In addition to quality, you pay for the dealer's information on the subject and his integrity. But the discerning collector usually prefers to buy in this manner, even if it is only on rare occasions; he then feels secure that he possesses something noteworthy. There are couples who plan their budgets to buy one fine antique a year, and when the time comes they get expert advice before making the decision. In this way, they acquire a collection that through the years constantly increases in value. Sadly, most people, with or without means, want to obtain their furniture quickly and at bargain prices, and do not take the time to study or to check carefully. They often end up with nothing of consequence and money thrown away.

There are times when something good is found in an off-beat place. But I assure you that when this happens the finder has the knowledge and instinct to recognize the exception amidst an array of what is often junk.

Numbers of small shops have good, well-selected stock. A fancy façade in an exclusive neighborhood does not guarantee a knowledgeable owner. Often the very grand-appearing shops do not have quality antiques, because the owner has stocked his shop with late imports and glorified pieces, not always deceitfully but through ignorance or lack of careful examination when he himself bought.

It is not easy to pick up a good antique at bargain prices today. Some years ago remarkably fine furniture could be found in country cabins or in modest homes in the city. With the introduction of new styles, the wealthy would often discard their old pieces in a rush to acquire the latest-fashion furniture. The impact of the Victorian period was so strong that this practice occurred extensively in the middle and late nineteenth century, particularly in the affluent industrial sections and the plantation areas. Residents were quick to bestow their old furniture on a domestic or a needy person, who in most cases took great pride in ownership. Consequently, numbers of people interested in preserving or collecting things of the past have scoured the country looking for such articles—more profitably in the South than in New England, since New Englanders were usually more thrifty and held on to their possessions rather than follow the fashion. What amazing furniture was to be found—sideboards, tables of various sorts, serving tables, beds, and desks—the whole in fair condition, although sometimes a damaged piece had been given away instead of being repaired. Once I saw a New York mahogany Pembroke table for sale, its many pieces tied in a neat bundle, and when it was purchased and assembled not one piece was missing, not even the smallest round of beading. Chairs were not found as frequently as other articles, because they had received continual hard use. On one occasion, when my husband and I were welcomed into a small cabin after asking if the occupants had any old things they would like to sell, we felt our way around a room that was shielded from any outside light by solid shutters at the window. The only illumination was the glow from the flickering wood fire, which was never extinguished, night or day, winter or summer. My husband said that he thought he had found a Chippendale piece in the darkness, and I asked if the occupants would please open the shutters. They did, and sure enough, there stood a handsome mahogany Chippendale side table with two long drawers, bearing some of the original bail handles. He had recognized the piece by feeling the sturdy, square chamfered legs typifying the Chippendale style. We purchased it for ten dollars, a large sum in those days. On our way home, we stopped at a well-known cabinetmaker's shop to check our find, and ascertained, on examining it in strong light, that it was of American origin, circa 1775. This took place on a late Saturday afternoon. Early Monday morning a man appeared in a taxi at our house outside the city and informed me he had heard that we had a Chippendale side table and he was authorized to offer me three hundred dollars for it. After a few minutes' hesitation, I accepted his offer and then asked how he knew I had the piece. He had been at a sale of fine furniture in Virginia and overheard two dealers discussing a Chippendale table someone had told them about that had just been found in Savannah. They were making plans to come down to buy it. He took an earlier train and, it turned out, preceded the two by several hours. I learned later he sold it for thirty-five hundred dollars to a wealthy client of his. This did not disturb me in the least, since I had no such outlet. The two dealers had been alerted by the cabinetmaker we had shown it to.

In order to be sure that the owners of the table had not been taken advantage of, we made friends with them and supplied food and medicine over a long period. During hard times, many pieces of this kind stood the chance of being destroyed; buying them often preserved them. I tried on numerous occasions to buy a curly-maple-and-cane Grecian bench that I had seen sitting on a porch. The owners refused to part with it, since the husband rested on it after he returned from work. Later, when I no longer saw it in its accustomed place, I inquired and was told it had been burned for firewood. Money from a sale would have bought many times that amount of firewood.

These extraordinary finds are still available, but at realistic present-day prices. Good furniture comes on the market at estate sales and with changes of taste. Because the prices are usually high, one must take extra precaution to be certain that the quality is commensurate with the price. There are, as has been stated previously, large numbers of nineteenth-century reproductions of eighteenth-century pieces and many glorified or assembled pieces in circulation. One must be alert and informed to spot them. Certain classes of furniture are copied more than others—for the obvious reason that since they are in more demand additions and alterations are comparatively easy to contrive. In my work as an appraiser, I have seen alarming quantities of deceptive furniture—articles bought, unfortunately, in good faith. Describing some actual fakes I encountered may help prospective buyers be more conscious of what to suspect.

Of all forms of furniture, the small tripod table or candle-

Sheraton-style tripod tilt-top table, American,
made in the South, circa 1815.
It is of the period and completely authenticated.
Mahogany, reeded pedestal terminating in tripod legs.

stand probably has been abused more than any other. Genuine period tripod or tilt-top tables are rare, and small occasional tables, always in demand, can be disposed of readily to an unsuspecting buyer. There are many ways to accomplish the fake. The one most seen is the marriage of a top with an old tripod form from a fire screen or part of the front post of a fourposter bed.

The fire or pole screen, which was designed to keep the

heat off a lady's face when she was sitting by the fire, was very fashionable in the late eighteenth and early nineteenth century. It may be that women are less conscious of the heat, or that the fires are not so hot; at any rate, the popularity of fire screens has diminished, and many are now converted into tripod tables. Since they were designed to protect the face of a seated person, the height of the shaft is considerably lower than that of an authentic tripod table. Actually, eight inches must be added to give the required height of twenty-six inches, and the join can sometimes be detected because the grain of the wood is different. There are times, too, when a low table is desirable by a fire or in front of a settee. In one instance, I found that the carved pedestal of sixteen inches attached to the tripod base was as it originally came from the pole screen. The giveaway was at the top of the pedestal where plugs were found filling in the holes that held the mechanism for the original sliding screen, and in a round piece of wood that was attached to the bottom of the top, which, incidentally, was of new wood. The completed table was twenty and a half inches wide, twenty and a half long, and twenty-three high. A charming table at first glance, and a decorative addition to the room, but it did not qualify as an eighteenth-century antique table, which was what it was sold for.

There are fairly easy ways to spot the false tripod or tilt-top tables. The original tables varied from large ones with circular tops and cabriole legs to ones of candlestand size with round, oval, or lozenge-shaped tops. The whole must be of the same wood. Contrasting woods were seldom used. If the top is circular, whether plain, piecrust, or dish top, measure the diameter with the grain of the wood, and right across the grain. If it is original, there will be a difference of from three-eighths to three-quarters of an inch. This is because wood shrinks slightly across the grain as it ages, but never with the grain. The shaft of the tripod must be in one piece of timber, rising from between the legs to the tabletop. Lift a tripod table, spin it slowly in your hands, and note the grain of the pedestal; it should be all the same, and should run the length of the shaft.

In the house where I found the shortened tripod table, there was another clever fake—a pseudo-birdcage table. This is an eighteenth-century tilt-top table in which the tripod is joined to a top supported by an intervening device called a "birdcage," which consists of small, turned baluster pillars. The birdcage allowed the top to revolve. To see through the deception on this one did not take serious examination. In spite of the fact that it revolved, as most reconstructed ones do not, the birdcage was found to be of new wood and not handmade; the round top was of old wood and measured twenty-nine inches both ways. When I turned it over, I found a new bracing attached with new screws. Above a sixteen-inch-high turned pedestal, which extended to the birdcage, was the addition of a rough, round section of inferior wood, to give the table the correct height and an appearance of authenticity.

In the past forty years many small tilt-top tables have been made that somewhat resemble antique examples. They are usually twenty inches high, with plywood tops. Old tilt-tops were never less than twenty-six inches high, and their tops were of solid wood rather than plywood, which is, of course, a modern material. Antique tripod tables had a three-pronged wrought-iron plate that strengthened the joining of legs and upright shaft; be sure to check that it is still in place. Also, although it is a minor consideration, if the top tilts, it should have the original latch in brass on the finer tables, a wooden button on the simpler ones.

The tripod in greatest demand, and the one that brings the steepest prices, is the elaborate table in the Chippendale style called the piecrust table, where the rim of the circular top is scalloped, with deep carved borders. To achieve this, the early craftsmen used an extra-thick piece of wood to allow for the carving. When the carving on the edge was completed, the balance of thickness was cut away to make a flat surface about three-quarters of an inch thick. In their original condition, these are rare and valuable—a temptation to the glorifier. What he does is to take a plain circular top and glue additional wood on the edge in about thirty-two short pieces lap-jointed together, and then carve them to simulate an original piecrust design. In faking a tabletop that has a raised molding (called a dish top), no new wood is added, the plain rim is carved, and the rest of the tabletop is planed away to the unusual thinness of about a half-inch. A table that has undergone such treatment no longer rates as antique and, needless to say, is not a desirable purchase.

In many years of examining tilt-top or tripod tables, I have found very few where all parts began life together. Some—probably all—of the "antiques" mentioned above I have seen among tables for sale. Obviously, extra-special caution should be taken in selecting a tilt-top table.

It sometimes takes artful detection to find the exact truth of furniture that has been assembled from various old unrelated pieces. There is usually an awareness from the first glance, and certainly from a more prolonged second look, that the piece under observation is wrong, the proportions faulty, and the several different styles represented inconsistent. Here is a mahogany secretary-bookcase, in two sections, dominating the room and unlike anything seen before in books, museums, or private homes. What is it? Whoever reconstructed it intended it to be a piece of importance. It cannot be classified in any particular period, because elements of several are depicted. The balance is unwieldy. What a teaser! One is held in suspense. With a close examination

The assembled and reconstructed mahogany "secretary-bookcase"

of the lower part, one is shocked by the incompatibility of the extremely large, square, chamfered legs terminating in block feet. The body placed on these four twenty-nine-inch-high legs is divided into three sections. The two side ones open to form drawers; the center section is a panel of new

wood, the front of which drops to reveal a newly constructed interior fitted with pigeonholes, small drawers, and other desk necessities, against a serpentine back. The legs are attached to this body with corner fret brackets of new wood. Placed fully over this lower section is a slab of old mahogany with a beveled edge. Sitting on this is the upper section, constructed of a mahogany different from any of the rest of the piece, and mostly new wood. The back of the bookcase is a new piece of plywood, the paned-glass doors are obviously taken from an old bookcase and attached to new sides, and the cornice is new.

Can you solve the mystery, or are you still in suspense? I must admit that at first I was completely puzzled. But going over it all again, and later seeing a picture that reminded me of parts of this piece, I suddenly found the answer. It was constructed from a Regency pianoforte, which was no doubt found without a keyboard or usable works, and was consequently of little value. After arriving at this, it was possible to figure out the rest. The two side sections fitted with drawers were originally the panels on either side of the keyboard, whereas the keyboard had been replaced with the newly made desk section. The large chamfered legs must have been obtained from an old cabinet, and the upper bookcase section rebuilt from some old and some new pieces. This bastard was represented by the dealer who sold it as an eighteenth-century Chippendale secretary and priced accordingly, which should give the buyer just cause to be wary in purchasing costly pieces.

Small inlaid mahogany sideboards with tapering legs are another temptation to the faker, or reconstructor. Most people have small dining rooms and there is a minimum demand for large sideboards, no matter how good or well carved they are. Many small sideboards are completely reconstructed from old wood, and many reduced in size from large ones. Eighteenth-century English sideboards should have six legs, each made of one piece of wood from the floor to underneath the top. Inlaid bands or beading may hide a join to the leg, so check. Also the tops of Georgian sideboards were made from one piece of timber, which in many cases warped.

For this reason, the Victorians made their tops in two or three pieces, which resulted in splitting veneer if one or two boards warped. If a Hepplewhite- or Sheraton-style sideboard is found with a repair right along the top, it was probably made after 1860. Good tops of good sideboards overhang slightly at the front, sides, and back. Pull out drawers and look under the top to see if there is a join, which indicates that it has been reduced in size or is Victorian.

An owner proudly displayed a mahogany-inlaid Sheraton-style sideboard sold to her as a fine Virginia piece, circa 1790. Before checking the interior, one could see that it was made of several different pieces of mahogany and poorly constructed. The cabinetmaker who contrived it went all out and included everything desirable. It had a bow front, and quantities of satinwood inlay, shells, and bands. Beneath the frieze drawers were double doors in the center opening up to a cupboard, on either side were doors concealing bottle compartments, and at each end was a small cupboard to hold chamber pots. Sideboards with this last convenience usually had only one opening. Looking inside, it was found that the maker had expended no effort at all to conceal the fact that it was put together with odd bits and pieces. Some of the drawer and door fronts were from old sideboards, not all from the same one; the drawer sides and bottoms were made out of any old pieces of crates, packing boxes, and plywood. It was unbelievable. Did the person who put together this astonishing fabrication think for a minute it was going to fool anyone? I doubt it, but the fact is that it did. Possibly the owner of the shop from which it was purchased accepted it without question and intended no hoax when selling it to the present owner, who accepted his assurance and bought it without question or examination.

Once again, you can't be too careful, or too aware, for these "naughty" pieces abound in today's antique shops.

XII

Woods

Another useful factor in determining the origin and age of furniture is the wood or woods of which it is constructed. As already stated, the early cabinetmakers were practical men and, to a large extent, used the woods that were available— the timber from trees growing nearby or from logs shipped into the area by water. Overland transportation in the eighteenth and early nineteenth centuries was time-consuming and arduous. Only a few logs could be loaded on a cart at one time, and even with the prevailing low wages the cost of transportation was staggering. These conditions helped determine the primary and secondary woods a cabinetmaker selected for his furniture. Primary woods, the ones used for the exterior of the piece, usually consisted of the hardwoods available or fashionable at the time, and included walnut, mahogany, cherry, maple, satinwood, and others. Secondary woods—those that do not show on a piece of furniture— were predominantly oak, deal, and Scottish pine in the British Isles; in America, native woods were used. Finding woods on an article that were indigenous to a certain country or to a certain section of a country may indicate where it was constructed, although this is not always conclusive, since oak, which is commonly used in English furniture construction, is found on some American-made pieces. In England the species of oak used were *Quercus robur* and *Quercus sessiliflorum*. Red oak (*Quercus borealis*) and white oak (*Quercus alba*) were commonly used for chair and table frames and for fly rails in eastern Pennsylvania, adjacent New Jersey, and eastern Maryland. Even researchers in wood anatomy, testing the splinters, do not find it easy to distinguish the difference between these English and American oaks.

Occasionally, too, woods from a distant area, rather than those growing near at hand, were used for the secondary parts. In the coastal areas of the lower South, for instance, where cypress (*Taxodium distichum*) and longleaf pine (*Pinus palustris*) grew in such abundance that they were largely used for secondary structure, some mid-nineteenth-century furniture is found in which the secondary wood is white pine (*Pinus strobus*), from the Northeast United States. Advertisements in Charleston papers testify to the fact that quantities of white pine were being shipped into the port. And a descendant of Thomas Henderson (1818–1889), a Savannah cabinetmaker and undertaker, explains it this way. Henderson's coffins were shipped from the Northern states in white-pine cases, which he then used for structural parts in the furniture he was making. This kind of economy was observed in other parts of the country as well. Even mahogany was used as a secondary wood in localities where it was being imported at a reasonable cost. Duncan Phyfe used it often, reserving the finer grades for exterior cabinetwork.

The presence of a single wood in construction of antique furniture is not enough to establish the place of manufacture. Where there are two or more American woods, that does substantiate American origin and can help to pinpoint the place of birth in conjunction with other elements, such as regional preference for certain forms and patterns, the character of the carving and inlay, and general workmanship. But even workmanship cannot be accepted conclusively, because cabinet shops employed journeymen and apprentices who practiced in various places. Assigning an article of furniture to a specific maker is still more tentative, and often imaginary. Before one makes or accepts an attribution, evidence must be gathered from every available source. The surest testimony is that which was placed by the maker on the piece, such as an inscription, a signature, mark, stamp, or label. Next in conclusiveness is an original bill of sale, or documented history of ownership. As mentioned earlier, these assurances seldom exist, and for that reason positive identification is risky. Without such evidence one should state simply that the object under consideration *possibly* was made in a certain country, and *perhaps* in a particular area of that country. As one's knowledge grows and a fuller acquaintance is made with regional workmanship and materials, it can be more credibly stated that the object under examination was made in England, Scotland, Ireland, or America, and even in a specific locality, such as New England, New York, Philadelphia, or the Southern part of the United States. Unfortunately, it has become prevalent among some dealers and collectors to ascribe furniture, without documentary proof, to a particular cabinetmaker, one whose name is familiar because of recent publications or because furniture said to have been made by him demands high prices. Favor changes with time, and the same article of furniture is later attributed to another cabinetmaker, whose name is then in vogue. To repeat, use utmost caution before you make or accept any identification.

Walnut

Walnut was the principal primary wood used for English furniture in the early years of the eighteenth century, the period first considered in this book. The years 1690 to 1720 are referred to as the "later walnut period," which followed the early walnut period, 1660 to 1690. Previous to about 1650, walnut was used only sparingly. Great numbers of walnut trees, both the European variety (*Juglans regia*) and the black walnut (*Juglans nigra*), were planted in England about 1560, and had come into maturity by the middle of the seventeenth century. Cabinetmakers found this wood to be a more suitable medium than oak for the scrolls, twists, and curves in vogue during the time of Charles II and William and Mary, and it proved most satisfactory for fine carving. Walnut is less likely to chip than oak, and after thorough seasoning walnut is less affected by variations in climatic conditions than the majority of other cabinet woods. Thus walnut was used to such an extent that the trees grown in England were not sufficient to meet the increased demand. This scarcity of locally grown walnut was met by importations of walnut from the Continent (especially from France) and from Virginia. The European walnut (*Juglans regia*) was used for structural parts and for veneers. The branch figure, or swirl, of crotch walnut enriched plain surfaces. The veneer was cut from a knot or excrescence called a burr or burl and was highly figured. Another pattern for veneer was called "oystering." This was cut transversely from stumps and crotches, producing a grain of rings that resemble the markings of the oyster shell, a highly decorative surface.

Trees that have grown in open ground may produce timber marked by striped, waved, or mottled figures. Irregular growths, such as crooks, forks, and stumps, yield prized veneers. Veneering was used for its rich warm effect on flat surfaces of cabinetwork, providing intricate figures on the fronts of desks, chests of drawers, and clock cases, and in the splats of fiddle-back chairs.

The principal disadvantage of the European variety of walnut as a structural material is its susceptibility to attack by larvae of the common furniture beetle. Seat furniture of the early and middle eighteenth century is frequently found with parts so entirely netted that only the outer polished surfaces remain—literally a shell. Black walnut was more prized, because it possessed the decided advantage of withstanding the damaging effects of the furniture beetle—a considerable asset in the British Isles. Quoting from John Evelyn's *Sylva*, published in England in 1664: "This black bears the worst nut, but the timber is much to be preferred; and we might propagate more of them if we were careful to procure them out of Virginia, where they abound. . . ." Evelyn recognized that the black walnut came from Virginia, where, he stated, there were three or four sorts, and that it was called in England by its correct name, "Virginia walnut"—although it is seldom mentioned when the same wood appears in American furniture. Quantities of this wood were exported to England from before 1700 and on. Extant bills of lading preserved in the British Museum testify to the source of the shipments, as do such advertisements as one in the *Daily Post* of London, August 30, 1731, for "Virginia Wallnutt-tree chairs." American walnut is moderately hard, and more difficult to work than European walnut. It has a fairly coarse but smooth texture, and is darkly colored. The name "black" comes from the color of the bark on the tree; the color of the sapwood is almost white, and the heartwood ranges from a light tan or grayish to a very dark brown. This wood was used for work in the solid, while most European walnut was customarily used for veneers.

Many other woods were used in England during the Queen Anne period. Oak was especially popular in the rural sections; pine, lime (the linden tree, *Tilia europaea*), and chestnut were used for elaborate carving, especially on mirror frames, and were often covered with gilt. They also served as groundwoods for veneer or lacquer, as did oak. Pear, beech, elm, and yew were employed in much the same way as pine, and largely by country joiners.

Because America was being colonized during the period in which walnut was introduced into England and for use in European furniture, few of the earlier colonists were acquainted with it; besides, circumstances did not permit the expression of cosmopolitan tastes. It was not until the end of the seventeenth century that the walnut period began in America. In New England there was very little, and it appeared chiefly in finer articles; but walnut continued to be used south of New York throughout the Colonial period, even though mahogany became extremely popular. Many Philadelphia tall chests of drawers and chairs were made of walnut in the Chippendale style. This wood was carefully selected for its handsomely figured grain. In Pennsylvania and southern New Jersey, walnut was a favorite from the end of the seventeenth century, and its popularity continued till as late as 1796. Its use in Philadelphia was so extensive that prices of furniture forms were quoted for walnut as well as mahogany. Rural Pennsylvania craftsmen continued to work in walnut throughout the nineteenth century. It was frequently used in western Pennsylvania and western Maryland, as well as Virginia, North Carolina, and inland Georgia and South Carolina, right through the nineteenth century. Less important was white walnut (*Juglans cinerea*), or butternut, native from New England down to Maryland. This wood is open-grained, light brown in color, and without much figure. It is often seen in country-made pieces, or on the sides and backboards of case furniture.

Mahogany

Mahogany began to supersede walnut in general use in England and America during the second quarter of the eighteenth century, although walnut made a reappearance about 1830 and was used extensively in both countries all during the Victorian period.

Spanish mahogany had been known in England for more than a century. It attracted the attention of a carpenter on board Sir Walter Raleigh's ship, in the exploration of Guiana in 1595. But before 1721 it was rarely used because of its high price. In that year the British government passed an act abolishing the heavy import duties on practically all the timbers from British colonies in North America and the West Indies. The purpose of the act was to increase supplies of timber for shipbuilding, but cabinetmakers naturally took advantage of the lower prices and one of the results was to stimulate trade in mahogany. Between 1725 and 1750 walnut and mahogany were of equal popularity in London. As the supplies of mahogany increased and its many fine properties were revealed, it generally supplanted walnut as the fashionable wood for furniture. Mahogany was superior to walnut in several ways, the major ones being that it possessed strong resistance to decay and was not liable to attacks of the woodworm. The great width of the boards made it ideal for tabletops, cabinet doors, and similar pieces. Being a strong wood, it affected mid-eighteenth-century furniture design, which is evident in rococo- and Chinese-style chair backs. Not the least of its assets, the beautiful patina of mahogany improved with use, and it was less apt to scratch, crack, or warp than were other woods.

It is possible that mahogany was in general use in America before it was widely used in England. Tradition has it that some mahogany appeared in furniture at the end of the seventeenth century. An inventory of 1708 states that the stock of Charles Plumstead, a cabinetmaker of Philadelphia, contained "2 mahogany planks," among others, and about this time William Till, a joiner of Philadelphia, owned "Mahogany Board . . . 209 feet . . . and Mahogany Scantling . . . 42 feet. . . ." The types of mahogany found in English and American furniture during the second half of the eighteenth century were from Cuba and Santo Domingo (*Swietenia mahogani*) and from Honduras (*Swietenia macrophylla*). There were many places in the West Indies and Central America, including the Spanish colonies, from which the timber was smuggled into England by way of the British settlements, in order to avoid the duty on foreign wood. The mahogany regarded with the highest esteem is generally known as Spanish (*Swietenia mahogani*), and was obtained principally from the Islands of Santo Domingo and Cuba, the finest being that from Cuba. This is of great weight, hardness, and closeness of grain. When it is worked, minute white flecks of a chalky character appear in the wood. As was natural, the finest and largest trees near the coast were cut first and exported, and thus the early mahogany furniture of England and America is of surpassing beauty in color and texture. As the supply on the coast was depleted, it was necessary to go farther inland for the larger trees, which resulted in greatly increased transportation costs. To avoid the extra expense, mahogany was imported from Honduras via the Bay of Campeche. This Honduran mahogany (*Swietenia macrophylla*) differed materially from the Spanish mahogany in that it was of more open grain, inferior color, and lighter weight. Occasionally it had a rippled figure. In both the Honduran and the Spanish mahoganies, the wood from the butt log is deeper in color and the figure is much more marked than in other mahogany. Honduran mahogany varies in color from pale reddish-tan to medium red-brown shades, although darker tones may occur. In contrast to the majority of West Indian mahoganies, which darken with exposure, the Honduran wood fades to golden or even decidedly grayish tones; it is also characterized by a more open texture, a straighter grain, and a greater softness. Either black or white deposits may occur in the vessels, but the former is more common. The finest Honduran timber was more showy in its markings than the woods obtained from the West Indies; it appeared with stripe, roe, mottle, fiddle-back, crotch, and swirl figures, making it a valuable medium for veneering. Flame veneering is a term referring to the character of the grain, such as that of the "pair of trousers," the name given to the first branch or crotch of the tree. Another, much sought after figure was the mottled—often called "plum pudding"—mahogany. The plum-pudding figure appears in a relatively small number of West Indian mahogany timbers, as a result of some external agency by which the wood is marked with chemical deposits.

The principal sources of a third commercial type of mahogany, African (*Khaya ivorensis*), were the Gold, the Ivory, and the Nigerian Coasts of Africa. African mahogany did not appear in Europe until about 1830, at which time a substantial amount of it was obtained and manufactured into furniture. It is similar to the western species. The logs measure from fourteen to thirty-six feet in length and from three to five feet in thickness; they yield longer and wider cuttings than any other type of mahogany. The wood when cut has a color of salmon pink, but with exposure to air and light, it changes to a pale reddish-brown. It is, as a rule, of a lighter texture, and has slightly larger pores than other mahogany, but African mahogany is more lavishly figured and is often converted into veneers. The figure, amazing in its variety and beauty, ranges from the simple, straight stripe to the rich and complex mottle, crotch, and swirl.

In America during the first quarter of the eighteenth century, other woods besides walnut and mahogany, such as cherry and maple, were employed. With the publication of Chippendale's *Director*, mahogany was used almost exclusively for the construction of the lavishly carved Chippendale furniture. Mahogany was a natural choice for American cabinetmakers because it was so accessible. In the 1760s, it usually took just under a month for a shipment of mahogany to reach the Southern coast cities of Charleston and Savannah from Port Antonio, Jamaica.

By the time of the classic revival of the Adam brothers, mahogany was too generally established in the public favor and had too many virtues to be abandoned. It was a superior medium for the special type of carved decoration known as *basso-rilievo*, in which the Adams delighted. In the Sheraton- and Hepplewhite-designed furniture, mahogany was used in lightly constructed chairs for the parlor and drawing room. Sheraton recommended a hard, straight-grained Cuban mahogany, stating it would "rub bright and keep cleaner than Honduras woods." He declared that "dining room furniture without exception was to be of mahogany as being most suitable for such apartments." Mahogany continued in its great popularity until after the middle of the nineteenth century.

Satinwood

The time of Adam is also referred to as the "age of satin-wood," since that wood was a close second to the favored mahogany. It was a time of colored woods and decorations on woods that produced dramatic effects. West Indian satin-wood (*Zanthoxylum flavum*) had been received in the British Isles as early as 1612, but it was not until the third quarter of the eighteenth century that it was used for English furniture both in the solid and as veneer. Many satinwood pieces were enriched by painted, instead of inlaid, decoration. When satinwood is freshly cut, it is pale yellow or yellowish-tan, taking on the richer, mellower tones found in the lustrous surfaces of old furniture. The texture is fine and uniform, the grain either straight or irregular; the latter accounts for handsome mottle and roe figures. Growth rings appear as lines in longitudinal surfaces and as rays in quartered material. With the exception of a few Baltimore and New York pieces during the Federal period, satinwood was not used to the same extent in America as it was in England. But in that period satinwood did play a prominent part in the pictorial banding and string inlays on furniture in the coastal areas of Massachusetts, New Hampshire, and Connecticut, in the Connecticut Valley, in New York, New Jersey, Pennsylvania, and Maryland, and in the South. The elaborate designs that resulted portray sunbursts, fans, lilies of the valley, garlands, eagles, shells, swirls, and many variations of those patterns. Satinwood was more costly than varieties of mahogany, and that may explain the small use of it in America for purposes other than inlay.

Exotic Woods

There were several other exotic woods used in England during the Adam period. One popular kind was harewood (*Acer pseudo-platanus*), also called sycamore. It had frequently appeared as an inlay material prior to its adoption as a principal cabinet wood when Robert Adam's influence first became apparent. The popularity extended to Ireland. Some of the finest pieces of Dublin origin were veneered and inlaid with harewood. This wood varies in color from yellowish-white to light tan with a yellow cast. It is comparatively hard, with a fine even texture and lustrous surface. A decorative fiddle-back grain is characteristic, though occasionally this is replaced by more pronounced curly markings. Rays appear distinctly in the usual quartered veneers. At times the natural color of the wood was treated with a chemical stain to make a soft, clear green tone or a soft purple tint. Other exotic woods were Amboyna, possessing a beautiful grain and mellow color, and esteemed as a veneer; tulipwood, admired for color and grain; holly and ebony, used for inlays.

In spite of the adoption of many new woods, mahogany retained its popularity during the Regency period for library, bedroom, and dining-room furniture. Rosewood also gained favor. The heavy scale and proportions of some of the mahogany and rosewood furniture of this period were alleviated by inlaying or veneering woods of lighter tones, such as Amboyna, kingwood, thuya, pollarded oak, and elm. And some of the finest Regency furniture was of satinwood, a holdover—or perhaps a revival—from 1790. Other decorative woods in use at this time were zebrawood, striped in a manner resembling the skin of the zebra on a ground of pale buff; and calamander, also known as coromandel wood, a product of several trees that are indigenous to Ceylon and

southern India. In appearance calamander is something between rosewood and zebrawood, with a red-hazel or choc-
olate-brown ground, figured with black stripes and marks.
Beech and deal were used for beds and other furniture; they
were painted or japanned, and at times grained to resemble
rosewood.

Rosewood

Rosewood began to be used in the late eighteenth century,
at first simply for bands of inlay in imitation of the French
Louis XVI furniture, but from the beginning of the nineteenth century it was used extensively for surfacing mahogany, oak, or cheaper pine carcasses. The great age of rosewood was from 1805 to 1840. There are many species of
rosewood. The Brazilian rosewood (*Dalbergia nigra*), also
called jacaranda and Bahia rosewood, came from Brazil, as
the name implies. The shades of color range from dark
brown and chocolate to violet, and it has conspicuous black
streaks. The source of East Indian rosewood (*Dalbergia lati-
folia*) was southern India and Ceylon. Its color is dark purple to ebony, with streaks of red or yellow, exceedingly fine
rays, and occasional crotches and swirls. Madagascar rosewood (*Dalbergia graveana*), also called Madagascar pali-
sander and French rosewood, came, naturally, from
Madagascar, and the color runs from dark to light rose-pink,
with pronounced lines of darker red. To a lesser degree,
Honduras rosewood (*Dalbergia stevensoni*), from Central
America, was used. The color is lighter than Brazilian, a
pinkish brown or purplish, and streaked with darker and
lighter bands. The wood is rather oily and slightly fragrant.
The oil from the rosewood tree is sometimes used as a base
for perfume.

Cherry

Cherry was used for furniture in America from Colonial times and continued as an important cabinet wood during the Early Federal period. American black or wild cherry (*Prunus serotina*) grows throughout the eastern half of America except in southern Florida. Supplies of this timber formerly rivaled those of America's light-brown walnut, but the species is no longer abundant. It is a light to dark reddish-tan color, moderately hard, straight in the grain, and usually rather plain in appearance. A mild type of growth-ring figure is displayed in some cuttings; rare instances of swirl, feather-crotch, or wavy figures enhance the choicest selections. The texture is fine and uniform, with pores so small as to be indiscernible without the aid of a lens. Burls are not uncommon, but these were not utilized until fairly recent times. Cherry was used especially in areas north of Pennsylvania and New Jersey. In New York and New England it appears in seat furniture, general cabinetwork, clock cases, and various other household articles. This local timber was particularly favored in Connecticut, for both simple pieces and fine furniture, including elaborately pedimented highboys, secretaries, and chests of drawers in the Queen Anne and Chippendale styles. In the Chippendale period in America, cherry was more often used than mahogany by Connecticut cabinetmakers.

Maple

Maple was selected for fine Colonial furniture in the New England area of northeast Massachusetts, southern New Hampshire, Rhode Island, and eastern Connecticut. There are numerous species of maple to be found in North America, some yielding timbers of excellent quality while others have little commercial value. The principal species in use since Colonial times has been the rock or sugar maple (*Acer saccharum*). It is an important source of maple sugar as well as timber. The wood varies in color from a light creamy-tan to a deeper pinkish-tan, and with the application of a plain varnish it acquires a light or medium yellowish-tan surface tone. It is hard and strong, with a fine even texture, and displays rather delicate deep-toned lines that heighten the effects of very mild growth-ring figures. The grain is generally straight, though decorative material is common in old furniture where the careful selection and matching of such wood is frequently apparent. The more usual grain types include fiddle-back, curly or "tiger stripe," and bird's-eye. Sugar maple is difficult to work, even in straight-grained timber, and the figured varieties proved even more obstinate, particularly difficult for the tools of Early American craftsmen. The wood is also subject to warping, and to splitting if nailed. It is one of the few woods in which vertical shrinkage may occur to a noticeable extent.

Maple, including bird's-eye, was used in England for picture frames. They date from about 1820 into the third quarter of the century. English maple had a full yellow color, and began as a cheap substitute for the costly satinwood, although in comparison it was a much lighter wood.

These woods were the most important and most frequently used primary furniture woods in England and America during the eighteenth and nineteenth centuries. There were others—such as beech, birch, holly, magnolia, pine, and red gum; and in some areas, pear, apple, and pecan—but most of the fine furniture was made from the walnut, mahogany, and others described above.

As stated earlier, secondary woods were for the most part timbers from the trees growing in the cabinetmaker's neighborhood, such as ash (especially in New York), chestnut (Rhode Island and eastern Connecticut), cypress (Southern coastal areas), oak, Southern pine (Pennsylvania, New Jersey, Maryland, Virginia, South Carolina, and Georgia), and tulip (New York, Long Island, New Jersey, the Hudson River Valley, Pennsylvania, and Maryland). It must be considered that almost any secondary wood might have been used in an isolated instance anywhere.

Warning: never jump to a conclusion about woods; check all possibilities.

XIII

Potpourri

Furniture in the Rough

As a person acquires more awareness of what to check when buying antique furniture, his confidence increases to the point where he feels he is capable of spotting good furniture in poor condition, and that by doing this he will be able to buy more cheaply. Buying antiques in disrepair requires additional knowledge: condition of furniture, even in the rough, remains of utmost importance. Not only is the cost of restoration expensive, but it is difficult to find an able, conscientious, skillful restorer or refinisher. Satisfactory restoration requires someone who will take the time to do the work carefully and correctly. And the present-day high cost of labor often makes it impossible to purchase enough time for the average restorer to work on a piece in an acceptable manner. A buyer may feel he has the ability to do the work himself. Restoring antique furniture has a certain fascination for anyone with a natural aptitude in the use of tools, be he beginner or expert craftsman. But an amateur is apt to carry this enthusiasm too far and overrestore the article by removing every scar and blemish and stripping it too deeply, because of the prevalent (and usually erroneous) idea that bare wood is the most beautiful. Such zealousness robs the piece of all evidence attesting to its age and long usage, and makes it look like a reproduction. Those who truly appreciate antique furniture cherish the indications of age. Working down to the bare wood may be necessary in some cases, but it is not always the best thing to do. Where the original finish is intact and in good condition—in spite of grime and dust on the surface—no attempt should be made to remove it. A thorough cleaning and polishing will often be sufficient, and thus the original patina is retained.

Novices often get carried away by what seems to be a find. For example, suppose you come upon what was originally a fine slant-top desk, priced at five dollars. The feet are gone, both the slant top and one drawer front are missing, and in addition it requires tightening, regluing, cleaning, and refinishing. What will you have when all the restorations and replacements have been made and many hours of time and materials expended? Nothing but an article of rebuilt furniture, which has no value as an antique. Remember that collectors do not consider a piece of antique quality if its replaced parts amount to more than 10 percent of the entire piece, or if its original shape or design has been altered.

When one begins to look for articles in the rough, it may be difficult to recognize the value of an untouched piece because of its condition or the surroundings in which it is found. Often it is crowded in with other pieces and stored in a place where the light is poor. Once when I was rummaging around in the back storage room of a shop, I spotted a table hanging among other pieces from the wall. Even in that awkward position and dim light, it appeared to have some merit. I asked the owner to lift it down and place it in the light. The wood was impossible to identify at first glance, because it had been extensively bleached by weather. Since it was priced reasonably, I bought it and after further examination was happy to find that it was constructed of solid mahogany and made somewhere along the Southern coast around 1790. Coats of dirt and dust, finish that is badly checked or cracked, coverings of several layers of paint, and a rough and scarred surface can disguise the true identity of a piece; many parts may be missing and it may need considerable repair—all of which can confuse the untrained buyer. When, through experience, your eye is geared to recognize the good from the inferior, then you can decide if something can be done with an article or if it is utterly hopeless.

Here is a check list to use when you look at furniture in the rough. After bringing the article into the light and wiping off as much of the dust and grime as you can, proceed as follows:

1. Look for missing parts.
2. Check for necessary repairs.
3. Examine the part where the drawer sides meet the front, and note the construction of these joints. If they are well-fitted dovetails or another type of joint, you may assume the rest of the piece is well constructed and of equal quality of workmanship.
4. Check the piece for loose joints by shaking it.
5. Test the wood for hardness with your fingernail or with the point of a knife blade—unless, of course, the wood is obvious. Test it in several places; there is the possibility that various kinds of wood may have been used in construction.
6. If the piece is covered with old paint, ask for permission to scrape off a small, out-of-sight section with a knife blade. By checking the edges of the spot scraped you can determine how many coats of paint it has had. Early American prim-

itives did not have a finish of any kind. At some time or other, as the furniture continued in use, much of it received a coat of paint, which was later followed by others. Some pieces may have been given as many as seven or eight applications. The ability of wood to take a good finish may also be tested, after scraping, by wetting the spot.

Techniques of refinishing and restoring are a personal matter. When you ask several people about methods, each will describe a different approach to the job. There are a number of factors to be considered, such as the species of wood involved, the extent of cleaning to be done, and the tools and paint and varnish removers that are needed. A person with knowledge in the field of restoration will give you the answers. Fortunately there are excellent books on the subject, written by people who have proficient knowledge gained from working extensively on antique furniture. These books, some of which are listed in the Bibliography, are of invaluable assistance. Even if you do not desire to do over the furniture yourself, it is good to have some familiarity with restoration techniques, to enable you to direct the professional you hire to do the job correctly and as you wish it done. There are no short cuts in good refinishing: each step, from removing the old finish to the final rubdown, must be followed in order; each must be properly completed before proceeding to the next one. With most finishes the work is not too difficult, but it is necessary to follow directions carefully and to have the patience to take the time to do the work well.

Sales and Auctions

Previously it was suggested that until you knew what to check when buying antique furniture, it would be wise to engage an appraiser to look at a piece under consideration or buy from a dealer who would stand behind the purchase by giving you a guarantee of what the piece is. Now, with study and more experience, you may wish to branch out on your own, not only looking for antiques in the rough but attending auctions, with the hope of discovering something extraordinary. There is a certain aura of excitement about all auctions, from the folksy country sales to the auctions held at large-city galleries. It is easy to get involved in the exhilarating atmosphere as you watch the people milling around, looking and discussing the forthcoming sale and hoping to obtain a bargain. Enthusiasm mounts and caution is abandoned. Before attending an auction with a serious idea of buying, there are certain preparations that it is wise to take. To begin with, you should have some idea of what you are looking for, what price that particular article is bringing on the current market, and what price you are pre-pared to pay. The price range of a piece can be ascertained by checking shops beforehand. On the average, the top price one should pay at auction is about two-thirds of what the same piece would bring in a shop. This theory is not always reliable. Much depends on the auction itself. What people the auction has attracted, whether many good and desirable items will be on sale, the enthusiasm of the crowd, the state of the weather, and where the sale is held—these are just a few things that will affect the price that items will bring. Very unpredictable. A secretary-bookcase that was esti-mated to bring between four and six hundred dollars at an auction brought eighteen hundred, since there were two opu-lent women present who wished to own it and pushed the bidding up. On the other hand, an extremely fine article has gone for just a few dollars because it did not attract the people attending that particular sale. Study the catalogue before attending. Most auctions supply one in some form;

the small country sales may distribute a mimeographed sheet, while the big galleries sell, usually at a price of several dollars, a well-printed booklet with many photographs. Catalogues describe each item, although, it is important to know, not always completely and not always accurately. This is usually the result of natural error, not a wish to deceive. The majority of the catalogues have an introduction stating that the house is not responsible for the correctness or accuracy of any statement, or words to that effect. In most cases the catalogues do not state the condition of the articles. This brings up the necessity of thoroughly examining them before the auction. The time when they are on display is given. Take this opportunity to check any item you might be interested in. If you do not feel competent to do this, bring an authority in the field to assist and direct you. Be on the lookout during the exhibition and you will find the experts judging the furniture, turning it over, pulling out the drawers, looking at the backs—in fact, scrutinizing every aspect of it. They will look not only at the pieces they are interested in bidding for but at many others as well, to divert attention from where their interests lie. At the big auctions an authorized employee is usually available to provide estimated selling prices, which will give you some idea if a piece is in your range. The auctioneers at the big galleries get to be familiar with the regular attendants, know what they want, and know where to look for the bids. A tyro can find himself in the midst of experts and those who know the ropes. Beware. There is a system called "the knockout ring" that was prevalent in British galleries for a number of years. It worked like this. A combine was formed prior to the sale and a bidder was appointed, with instructions on what pieces he was to buy. It was understood that no one else in the combine would bid. If an outsider had the audacity to bid, the ring would run him up to such an exorbitant price that he soon learned his lesson: to buy from the combine after the auction. In this way, the knockout ring came to rule the important auctions, and only undesired articles were available to nonmembers. At the end of each sale, the ring members got together and held a second auction. The total amount realized from this wildcat auction was often much higher than the sum of the ring's purchases at the sale, and the net profits were divided among the members. Thus a member of the ring could make a tidy amount at an auction without participating at all. Several years back, there was a concerted effort to end this practice, and one of the newspapers spent time investigating the system and published a series of articles on the subject. In England the ring's power was reduced, and now many amateurs have become proficient at recognizing good pieces and like to bid for themselves. Although the ring was never as strong in America as in England, it still manages to survive and still operates at important sales. An owner of a fashionable antique shop told me with some pride that he had joined a bidding club, another term for the ring, and was able to get some especially good prizes at a sale of very fine Americana.

It is an interesting and entertaining experience to attend an auction, and at times profitable, but it is essential to keep on your toes and not get carried away by the excitement and fever of the occasion. There are people who attend the auctions weekly and get to know the regulars who are bidding, where their desires are directed, and when not to compete. In time these regular auctiongoers will become familiar with the customs and be able to acquire some good buys. In starting out on the auction trail, however, you must remember that you are contending with professionals.

Furnishing Your House

You can avoid unnecessary expenditure of time and money if you give thoughtful consideration to furnishing a room or a home before actually making any purchases. When furniture is carefully selected and placed in a proper setting, its natural attractions are enhanced. In assembling antiques to furnish your home, quality rather than quantity should be of major importance; start with a few good pieces rather than with many indifferent ones. Make a plan that includes what use is to be made of each room, what furniture is needed, which are the most important articles to obtain, what styles you prefer, and how much money you are prepared to spend; then adhere to this plan as closely as possible. Do not be in too much of a hurry to complete the plan. If you rush, you will not give proper attention to each piece. A wise person may wait for a long time to fill a certain spot. By taking your time and keeping your eyes open, you will learn new things about the subject; and mistakes will be kept to a minimum.

When making a plan, there are some basic style and design problems to keep in mind. For example, you may prefer one style to another; but combining styles, as well as woods, will result in charm and interest, and you will have a broader field of selection. Blending several styles prevents your house from looking like a museum confined to one style to display what was fashionable during a certain period. Avoid overcrowding, although the collecting instinct prompts accumulation and your pocketbook may permit it. If a certain article tempts you but doesn't fit into your scheme, refrain from buying it. Your house should not look like an antique shop either, cluttered with objects that can neither be seen nor used to advantage. One of the chief enjoyments in acquiring antiques is the satisfaction you derive from using them as they were intended by their makers.

There are some basic concepts of design that, if followed when planning your home, will result in a more harmonious surrounding. Thought should be directed to comparing the bulk of the pieces considered for use, especially when you are combining articles representing different periods and of different shape and line. For instance, think of the effect of placing a dainty Hepplewhite chair in front of a massive Chippendale-style secretary-bookcase. Tall pieces appear to better advantage when arranged in a broken line not of the same height. All the large furniture or all the small pieces should not be grouped together, but should be mixed and scattered around. Care should be observed about placing too large pieces in a small room, since this results in crowding, and nothing destroys the charm of a room more quickly. This can often be adjusted by judicious placing of the objects. Architectural affinities of furniture and the relationship of the furniture to the physical characteristics of the room are most important. When the grouping of furniture is achieved in a natural, obvious, and logical manner, the room has the air of being pleasantly lived in. A fireplace, if present, is regarded as the central point around which everything else in the room tends to be arranged.

These are ideas to keep in mind when you draw up your scheme, for they will suggest what pieces to consider when you buy. Many people have certain articles of furniture that they have inherited or been given, as well as pieces they may want to use because of sentimental attachment or necessity. Include these in the plan before buying additional furniture.

The above suggestions are to assist you in buying cautiously and economically. They are not to direct the fashion to be exemplified in your home. That is an individual matter and should portray your own taste and desires.

Furniture Care

After acquiring antique furniture, one must give it tender loving care to preserve it. This requires a schedule of dusting, cleaning, polishing, and waxing, and constant attention to proper humidity. Humidity is of particular importance because the wood should not become too dry or absorb too much moisture, which causes it to shrink or to swell. While keeping furniture in good shape is not difficult, it is necessary to give it proper regular care, and not omit it over long periods of time. The patina of furniture, a mellow richness of color and texture, is purely a surface condition and is, as has been discussed previously, a great asset to antiques. However, it is not only the surface of furniture that needs care but the interior as well.

In most households, dusting furniture is taken for granted, and done habitually; it aids in maintaining and improving the original beauty of the finish. The process of dusting removes the accumulation of dirt, grime, and mildew (especially evident in damp climates), and helps to polish fine finishes so that more drastic methods are unnecessary. Soft cloths should be used, and care taken to avoid catching loose pieces of veneer or inlay and pulling them off. If this happens, the detached pieces should be carefully preserved for regluing. Care must be taken also in using the vacuum cleaner. Articles designed close to the floor, legs, and feet are most vulnerable, not only to scratching and marring, but to having large sections of veneer knocked off.

There are instances when furniture acquires such a coat of grime that it cannot be removed by dusting alone but must be taken off by washing. This occurs often on dining-room chairs, where, in the passage of time, greasy fingers may leave marks that catch dust, or on furniture marred by oily and smoky fumes from kitchen or fireplace. There are several methods that can be resorted to, depending on how severe the damage is. For mild cleaning, wash the piece thoroughly with a soft clean rag dipped in warm water to which has been added a small amount of mild soap such as Lux or Ivory. Then wipe it dry with clean cloths. For badly soiled pieces, and varnished pieces, use a mixture of one quart of hot water, three tablespoons of boiled linseed oil, and one tablespoon of turpentine. Turpentine helps to cut the dirt, while the linseed oil lubricates, feeds, and polishes. Since this is an inflammable solution, it is imperative to use a double boiler to keep the mixture hot. Wet a soft cloth with the solution and polish with a soft dry one. In extreme cases it may be necessary to repeat the process. Where children are around, furniture is apt to become sticky from butter, syrup, or other sugary substances. To remove these, soak a soft cloth in warm water, fold into it—making a pad—a teaspoon or more of green soap, and rub the surface in a circular motion until it is covered by a lather. Then remove the lather with a cloth dampened in tepid water and dry and polish with a soft dry cloth, rubbing with the wood grain. Take caution when washing veneered surfaces to prevent the water from getting into the glue and loosening the veneer. If the veneer is not cracked, a small area may be washed and quickly wiped dry, but if the veneer is damaged in any way, it is best cleaned with a commercial product made for the purpose. After any cleaning job, the piece should be polished or waxed.

There are various opinions about the use of furniture polishes. Some professionals feel that an occasional rubbing with a furniture polish is advantageous but that an excess of oil polishes should be avoided, since they have a tendency to produce a dull and lifeless surface, which collects even more dust. When using commercial polishes, follow the directions on the container closely. With the majority of polishes, the most satisfactory method is to soak a piece of cheesecloth in hot water and wring it out; then, when the cloth is cool, apply the polish, which has been well shaken, sparingly. Clean the furniture by brisk rubbing. As the cloth becomes dirty, turn it and continue rubbing until the article is clean. Rub the surface with a soft dry cloth until a fingerprint will not be visible. There are several formulas for furniture polish recommended by experts. A mixture of one part boiled linseed oil and one part turpentine brightens the finish, removes a dull, foggy appearance, and helps to stop surface checking. The suggested use is once or twice a year on varnished and highly polished wood. Apply the mixture with a soft cloth, wipe off excess with a dry one, and polish with the grain of the wood. Another polish that may be used on various finishes—a polish that cleans as well as feeds the wood—is one part liquid paraffin and one part white gasoline or benzine, applied with a damp cloth and rubbed.

Waxing is usually considered preferable to polishing, since it has a more lasting and softer effect. Once wax is correctly applied, it lasts for a long time and its polish can be revived by rubbing the surface with a soft, lintless cloth. Additional wax should be applied only when it is needed, because when wax is applied too thickly it builds up and is a detriment to a good finish, becoming sticky in damp weather. Wax should always be applied to a finished surface. If it is applied to bare wood, grime works into it, and the grimy wax is almost impossible to remove if it becomes necessary to redo the piece. Always use a good paste wax, which is available in grocery stores. Most waxes come in yellow, but there are varieties colored brown, reddish-brown, and red to blend with different woods. Waxing is neither difficult nor involved. The equipment necessary is a good paste wax, a piece of heavy linen or closely woven cloth about ten inches square for applying the wax, and a tightly woven or hard cloth for final polishing. Place about two heaping tablespoons of wax in the center of your cloth and fold the cloth over it into a pad. Rub the entire surface of the article in a circular motion with the pad, leaving a thin coat of wax. Let the wax dry thoroughly, about thirty minutes, before polishing with the hard cloth. To repeat, additional wax should be applied only when it is needed. This is indicated when the surface does not polish after it has been rubbed with a soft dry cloth.

The surrounding atmosphere affects the condition of furniture, especially in climates with a wide range of temperature change, or in places where it becomes extremely dry. The dryness caused by furnace heat can be alleviated by placing pans of water on radiators, or on blocks over a register. If this is not feasible, pans of water may be placed under the furniture itself, and even in unused drawers. Humidity of from 40 to 60 percent is desirable. Some modern furnaces with electric fans have built-in humidifiers, and there are also available floor-model humidifiers in separate units at reasonable prices. Government statistics state that the average moisture in seasoned lumber varies from 6 to 14 percent according to weather and other climatic conditions; tests are based on a moisture content of 12 percent as normal. It is hard to believe that dry wood contains so much moisture. That wood lowers or raises its moisture content in accordance with the humidity of the place where it is located is, however, understandable. Furniture used in extremely dry places, such as in desert areas where the humidity is low, will crack or split and the glue will give way. This will happen, as well, to furniture in houses where the humidity is too low. Too much dampness is also harmful and causes swelling of drawers, mildew, mold, and loosening of glue. One wonders which is worse, too much dampness or too much dryness. Furniture imported from England that has been sitting for a century and a half in slightly heated rooms suffers in the extreme when it is bought and placed in overly heated American homes. Every precaution should be taken to give it the proper humidity before the veneer cracks and becomes damaged. The beauty and resulting enjoyment of well-cared-for antique furniture justifies the extra effort and time expended.

Furniture Beetles

When considering the condition and care of antique furniture, you must face the problem of holes made by the furniture beetle (*Anobium punctatum*), often falsely called "wormholes." Many people think, quite wrongly, that when these are found in an article of furniture, they prove it to be truly antique. Several stories told in antique circles center on this misconception. There is one about a wife who, when asked what her husband did, said his trade was boring wormholes in furniture to antique it. His skill was considered beyond detection. Another one relates that in a court case in which the antiquity of an article of furniture was being contested, the evidence failed to hold up against the expert testimony of an antique specialist in the United States Customs Service who, upon taking the stand, staged a simple demonstration. He put broom splints into the "wormholes" of the piece in question and pointed out how each one stood upright; he explained that since the holes left by the furniture beetle are exit holes, follow the grain of the wood, and run at all angles, this proved that the holes were man-made. There is still another story about the dealer who shot wormholes into furniture to antique it. Actually the holes caused by the furniture beetle do not prove that an article is antique, because these pests are as active today as they have been for hundreds of years. They are found all over the world, but fortunately not in any great number in the United States. It is not an asset to find beetle holes in furniture, and if the beetles are still active, strong countermeasures should be taken immediately. If a contaminated article is placed among other furniture, it is probable that all the surrounding pieces will become infected. This is a distressing problem that has occurred in museums. Since quantities of furniture are ravaged by the beetles, it is helpful to have some knowledge of their habits and the best measures to combat them.

The beetle, which is cylindrical, four to six millimeters long, and reddish-brown to dark brown in color, emerges in late May or June from cells immediately below the surface of the wood. Occasionally it is found crawling or flying in the house. Beetles occur in floors, rafters, and furniture of pine, and are also reported to have been seen in oak, beech, alder, and willow in England. They may attack any native American wood, but they prefer walnut, maple, and fruitwoods. One particular species of beetles likes chestnut. Chestnut was once a common forest tree in America, but early in the twentieth century it was all but wiped out by a fungus. The beetles went to work after the fungus killed the trees, but before the wood was cut. The "wormy chestnut" of the modern lumber trade is the product of these depredations.

The common furniture beetle usually infests sapwood indoors and heartwood outdoors. Wood that was attacked before it was cut can be recognized by the fact that some of the holes go straight through and others cut lengthwise. Furniture that has been infested will have only round holes that go in and then roam about inside the wood. The beetles may do so much damage that only the outer shell of a piece of furniture will remain. Wood in that condition is spongy and already broken, and should not be considered for your home no matter how reasonably it is priced.

One day after the male emerges from the wood, the female lays her eggs in a crevice in the wood or in the mouth of an old exit hole. She may oviposit one or more eggs in the crevice if it is sufficiently large. Eggs are not usually laid on a smooth surface, and wood with pores filled by paint, varnish, or other material is less likely to be infested than unfinished rough wood. The white, oval, lemon-shaped eggs are less than a millimeter long and show fine honeycombed sculpturing at one end, the remainder of the egg being smooth. Research shows that no egg hatched or hatching is impaired at humidities below 60 percent. The eggs hatch in six to ten days. The full-grown larva is about six millimeters long, is white with nearly black jaws, and has three pairs of five-jointed legs. On the dorsum are small brown spinules, set in double rows. These spinules enable the larva to gain purchase in the burrow. The results produced from the boring consist, for the most part, of small oval pellets. The larva pupates for two or three weeks in a cell immediately below the surface of the wood.

Emergence holes of the beetles are approximately two millimeters in diameter, varying with the size of the beetle. The shorter the life cycle, the more beetles produced and the more holes made. The main condition that favors them is abundance of food supply, which is more likely to be present in sapwood than in heartwood, a factor causing the rapid development of the pest. There appears to be considerable variation in the food supply, not only in different timbers but in different parts of one piece. At the same time, the more sapwood there is in the vicinity of a detected infestation, the more likely it is that the attack will be widespread. Rising moisture contents of wood in use, high prevailing atmospheric humidities, and mild temperatures are also conditions favorable to the pest, and consequently to a short life cycle. Cellars, cupboards under stairs, pantries, and unused attics are places where the common furniture beetle is likely to develop, if it does not already exist. And, except for pantries, it is in just such places that infected timber is most likely to be introduced. Logs, old packing cases, and timber from garden sheds, often full of beetles, are very commonly dumped in cellars with a view to later conversion to firewood. Attics and little-used rooms are where most people tend to store old furniture, or bargains bought from junk shops. Since these rooms are out of sight, the first two or three generations of furniture beetles may be produced before the presence of any infestation is detected, and by then it is possible that the population has spread over the whole house.

Generally, pieces of antique furniture purchased through a reputable dealer or firm are unlikely to be sources of infection. Although a piece may have been attacked by the furniture beetle at some time or other, its current presence would hardly fail to escape notice, and a specialist in the trade will probably have taken precautions to minimize the risk of infestation and deterioration while the article was on his premises. Bargains cheaply acquired, and gifts from friends and relatives, should never be given the benefit of the doubt. It is worthwhile to give them a very thorough dressing with one of the solvent wood preservatives, paying particular attention to all hidden surfaces, joints, crevices, and the like, before admitting the new acquisitions to a place among your existing possessions. A 5 percent pentachlorophenol treatment will control the beetle emerging from the wood for three to four years. But it is advisable to consult an expert exterminator to discover the extent of the active beetles. If they have spread over a large area in your home or shop, it will be necessary to seal up entire rooms for a period to treat them with gas.

Advice to the Novice

The novice collector is justified in feeling bewildered and discouraged when he considers a purchase of antique furniture. The many minute points outlined in this book to be checked and the many deceptive pieces on the market are reasons enough to dissuade a would-be buyer from acquiring antique furniture. But it is not as bad as all that. For instance, consider walking. If we stopped to review each movement and muscle necessary to put us in motion, the chances are we would never take the first step. So it is in utilizing the facts we have absorbed in determining the quality and condition of antique furniture. With time, study, and experience we gain confidence and intuition that automatically guide us to recognize at first glance whether the piece under consideration is good or phony. If there is the slightest suggestion that it is not right, then all that is necessary is to take the second look and inspect it diligently, using the information stored in your mind to check the necessary points. A very minor thing may make you aware that an article of furniture is not all it should be—replaced feet, classic inlay on a Chippendale chest of drawers, a complete lack of proportion. Whatever it is that makes you suspicious, the chances are that if there is one obvious faulty detail there are more deceptive features. A naughty piece cries out to you and sets your senses in motion. One important way to accustom your eye to correct pattern and style, and to good proportion, is to familiarize yourself thoroughly with the fine well-designed and well-constructed antiques in museums and reliable shops. Scrutinize them thoroughly and often, until your eye is trained to the extent that you can quickly see if a piece has been tampered with. Study design books of the various periods and styles. It takes patience to judge and buy wisely; even for those who have expert knowledge in the field of antique furniture, nothing can be taken for granted. Seriously review each factor previously described in this book for each piece of furniture you consider. The checking and patience pay off in the end, because your purchases will form a more worthy collection than if you acted precipitously. Thorough examination and attention are especially important when you are investing large sums of money. Occasionally there may be reasons to accept an article that is not exactly right; for example, if it is very inexpensive, or is needed to fill a particular space. But still be aware of what you are buying and for what reason, and consider it as a temporary placement to be exchanged for a better object in the near future.

Having the instinct and knowledge to discriminate between the good and the bad is not only of value when you are buying but adds immeasurably to your enjoyment and appreciation of antiques in general. It gives you a wider knowledge and awareness of history and an eagerness to learn more about the creations, the social background, the methods, and the aims of those who raised craftsmanship to the level of the fine arts. You get to know intimately the customs and habits of people who lived during the time of Queen Anne, or the Georgian era, or in the long reign of Victoria. What life in America was like in the early years becomes evident when you study the furniture that the early settlers used. Your scope of interest is no longer limited to present-day living, but stretches back into the past and gives added enrichment. This intense interest in the past is evident in the many houses in America, in England, and on the Continent that are being restored, furnished, and opened to the public, and the large crowds of visitors the houses attract.

All of these are motives to encourage a desire to detect

antique furniture. A prime advantage is the many friends you make through a shared hobby or interest and the pleasure it brings to your life.

The pastime of collecting is not a recent development. The ancients were collectors of the rare, curious, and beautiful. The Medicis were renowned for filling their houses with fine arts of every kind. This is a hobby that has engaged many great, as well as humble, people. It has been said, "Blessed is the man who has a hobby." I think those most blessed are the collectors of antiques, curios, old prints, coins, medals, rare books, porcelains, and furniture. The true collector is not merely a gatherer of things, indifferent to the guidance of a discriminating taste. When he finds an object, he considers it from many angles: its historical value, its significance in the development of the arts, the tales it might provoke, its value as a work of art, and its workmanship. The person who is indifferent to the whys and wherefores of things, and uninterested in any effort to discover the story of an object, bored by its history and unappreciative of its beauty, will hardly become a collector.

As a would-be collector, you may feel that it is an undertaking that requires special qualifications. You may ask, How can I hope to become a collector with so little knowledge of the subject? And you may also be afraid that the objects you want will cost too much and the real bargains will have vanished from the market by the time you get there. The question may be answered with the axiom: "The way to learn to collect is by collecting." As a collector, you will come into contact with the objects themselves and that contact leads to connoisseurship; at the same time, it is one of a collector's pleasures. In addition, you will also need to consult writings on the subject. Comparative study will increase interest and confirm or correct your personal deductions and opinions. The intuitive sense mentioned earlier will carry you a long way, but real connoisseurship is based upon sound knowledge.

As for your fears about price and availability, it is true that supremely fine examples of antiques are seldom picked up for a song. However, you should not get discouraged because you cannot collect museum pieces. There is still an open field of worthy prospects, and you will soon learn where you can search for and find things with your limited means and rejoicing heart. It adds to the pleasures of collecting that though you might know where to seek out treasures, it is possible to come across a find in the most unexpected place. You never know where something surprising will turn up.

The search is on. Good hunting!

A Glossary of Terms

ACANTHUS. A spiny- or toothed-leaf architectural ornament resembling the leaves of the acanthus (*Acanthus spinosa*) plant. It appears on the Corinthian capital and is the most widely used plant form in the decorative arts.

AMORINI. Cupids, a motif much in favor during Elizabethan times, the latter half of the seventeenth century, and again after 1750. Also termed "putti."

ANTHEMION. A decorative ornament in the form of stylized honeysuckle (camomile), flowers and leaves, originally derived from classical architecture.

APRON. The piece of wood that adjoins the base of cabinet structures. It may be straight or shaped. The term also applies to the band of wood with or without a drawer under a table-top and below the seat rail of a chair.

ARMOIRE (French). A clothespress. A large wardrobe or movable cupboard, with doors containing shelves and hanging space.

ARM SUPPORT. The vertical or curved upright supporting the front end of chair arms.

ART NOUVEAU (New Art). Spans period between about 1885 and 1914. A style of fine and applied art current in the late nineteenth and early twentieth centuries, characterized chiefly by curvilinear motifs derived from natural forms.

ASTRAGAL. A small convex molding of rounded surface.

BALL FOOT. A rounded foot mainly employed during the late seventeenth century as a terminal to cabinets or to the turned legs of tables, and so on.

BAMBOO TURNING. An execution in a softwood, usually painted or japanned, simulating the natural appearance of bamboo. It was used on Sheraton, or American fancy Sheraton, dating from the late eighteenth century, and in the English Regency period. Derived from Chinese design.

BANISTER-BACK CHAIR (American). A chair influenced by a mixture of Flemish and Spanish styles, made in America during the early eighteenth century. The back comprises a series of half-round (split) uprights called spindles and the top is surmounted by a carved cresting.

BAROQUE. An architectural style of Italian origin characterized by conspicuous curves, broken scrolls, and architectural decoration. In vogue in architecture, furniture, ceramics, and so forth, during the sixteenth and seventeenth centuries, until superseded by the rococo style at the beginning of the eighteenth century.

BASIN STAND. An eighteenth-century bedroom stand with a circular hole in the top to hold a basin and ewer. Sometimes triangular to fit into a corner.

BEAD. A molding resembling a string of beads.

BEAU BRUMMELL. An American term for a gentleman's fitted toilet table made during the latter half of the eighteenth century. The term is meaningless, since such tables were in use long before 1778, when George Brummell was born. Chippendale called his version a shaving table in the third edition of the *Director*, and Hepplewhite illustrated his design in the *Guide* of 1788 as a Ladies' Dressing Table.

BENTWOOD FURNITURE. First made by Michael Thonet, of Boppard-Am-Rhein, who began experimenting with this form in the 1830s. Thonet moved to Vienna and developed the process by which wood, usually beech, was heated with the aid of steam or boiling and bent in wooden molds. He started a factory for mass production in 1849. He also made chairs in parts, which could be assembled at their destination with the aid of a few screws.

BERGÈRE (French). An armchair with upholstery enclosing the sides from arms to seat, and supplied with a soft loose cushion resting on an upholstered platform.

BEVEL. A plain chamfer or cutting away of the edge in which two plain surfaces meet.

BIDET (French). A small stand fitted for bedroom toilet use. It has a violin shape, and holds a metal or pottery basin. Principally used for feminine hygiene.

BIEDERMEIER-STYLE FURNITURE. A German style of the first half of the nineteenth century, based on French Empire, but plainer and less ostentatious. Emphasis was on comfort rather than display. The name derived from two characters in a Berlin journal, Biedermann and Bummelmeier, who satirized bourgeois philosophy.

BLOCK FOOT. A square, vertical-sided foot at the base of a straight untapered leg.

BLOCK FRONT. Refers to the front of a desk, chest of drawers, and the like, that has three vertical divisions of equal width, a sunken one between raised ones. Regarded as an American innovation of the eighteenth century, it originated in Holland and Germany. It reached its fullest development with the case furniture made by the Townsend-Goddard family of Newport, Rhode Island.

BOMBÉ (French). Describes the swelling or convex surface on the front and sides of case furniture. The term is derived from the fact that the curves round outward, "like a bomb."

BONHEUR-DU-JOUR (French). A small writing table with the rear portion surmounted by a small cupboard for writing equipment, toilet articles, or bibelots.

BOSTON ROCKER (American). A type of rocking chair based on the Windsor chair, dating from about 1825.

BOW FRONT. The front of a chest of drawers, table, or sideboard that curves outward from either end. Also called swell front.

BRACKET FOOT. A foot of bracket shape employed to support

cabinets and chests of drawers. Introduced about 1690 and continued in use.

BREAKFRONT. A piece of furniture, such as a wardrobe or a bookcase, in which the central section projects slightly beyond the two flanking parts.

BUHL. A nineteenth-century word describing tortoise-shell and brass inlay furniture in the style of André Charles Boulle (1642–1732), the French cabinetmaker.

BUN FOOT. A flattened, turned ball foot introduced in the latter half of the seventeenth century. In America it is termed a ball foot.

BUREAU. The American chest of drawers is often called a bureau, whereas in Europe the term is reserved for a writing desk.

BUTTERFLY TABLE (American). A table in which leaves of the top are supported by two winglike swinging brackets. American in origin, it dates from about 1700 to 1750. Made only in New England—Connecticut, parts of Massachusetts, and possibly Rhode Island. Rare. Scarce woods used were maple or cherry for the top, and various native hardwoods for legs, stretchers, and other parts of the base. In original state they were painted.

CABRIOLE LEG. A leg that curves out from the seat of a piece of furniture and in again before reaching the foot, where it is again parallel to the seat. Resembles a conventional animal leg.

CAMPAIGN FURNITURE. Portable furniture—chairs, tables, beds, and chests especially intended for military use, and for traveling. Most surviving examples date from the Napoleonic Wars, and were used by high-ranking officers.

CANTERBURY. A piece of furniture designed to hold music or publications, or other articles.

CARCASS. The body of a piece of furniture, to which the veneers and finish are applied.

CARVER CHAIR (American). A chair with arms entirely made up of turned sections fitting into each other. The name is said to be derived from a chair of this kind in the possession of Governor Carver of the Plymouth Colony. A slightly more elaborate variety is sometimes termed a Brewster chair. About 1650.

CARYATID. A conventionalized female figure, supporting an arch or entablature. In the early seventeenth century it was found on chests and cupboard fronts. Again popular from the close of the eighteenth century through the Empire period.

CASE FURNITURE. Furniture fitted with drawers or shelves designed to be placed against a wall.

CAVETTO. A round concave molding, generally described as a hollow.

CELLARET. A deep drawer or tray for bottles in a sideboard, or an article of furniture designed to hold bottles.

CHAMFERED. Describes a surface or edge that has been smoothed off, beveled, or cut away from the square.

CHESTERFIELD. An overstuffed couch with arms as high as the back.

CHIFFONIER. A high chest of drawers, ranging from a small piece for odds and ends to a full-sized bedroom piece to hold clothes.

CHINOISERIE. Objects produced in Europe and America in the Chinese style or of Chinese inspiration. The term is never applied to anything produced in China itself.

CIRCA. Abbreviated c. About—used especially in approximating a date, such as c. 1750.

CLAW-AND-BALL FOOT. A carved detail of ancient origin resembling an animal or bird claw clasped round a ball.

CLUB FOOT. A knoblike foot formed as a continuation of a cabriole leg; less fat than a pad foot but otherwise similar. In use from about 1705 to late in the eighteenth century.

COCK BEADING. An astragal molding, small and applied to the edges of drawer fronts. About 1730–1800, following the use of lip-edged drawers.

COLONIAL. Pertaining or belonging to a colony. Architecture and furniture of America was called Colonial until the Revolution, when America was no longer a British colony. The term is erroneously used in describing furniture after 1776 in America.

COMMODE. The commode proper in England and France during the eighteenth century was a highly decorative piece of furniture—low, provided with drawers, and sometimes with cupboards. Falsely called a chest of drawers. The distinction: a chest of drawers is essentially bedroom furniture, and a commode was usually intended for the drawing room. Also a simple small cabinet fitted for bedroom use.

COMPO. Abbreviation of the term "composition," a casting material of whiting, resin, and size, similar to gesso. While still plastic, the mixture was pressed into molds and left until it hardened. It was first used by the Adam brothers for making prefabricated architectural ornament in imitation of plasterwork.

CORNICE. The molded or decorated projection that forms the crowning feature at the top of case furniture.

COROMANDEL SCREENS. Colorful folding screens of incised Chinese lacquer panels mounted on a wooden frame usually eight feet high and made in up to twelve leaves. They owe their name to the fact that they were transhipped on India's Coromandel Coast.

CROCKET. A medieval ornament, almost always suggesting a plant form and used especially on vertical and steeply inclined surfaces. Revived during the Victorian period.

CURULE CHAIR. A backless stool, often folding, with curved legs, derived from the Roman X-shaped stool. It was a popular furniture form during the Renaissance and appeared again during the early nineteenth century. It was a design adopted by Duncan Phyfe.

CYMA CURVE. A wave curve—double C or S. Also referred to as "the Hogarth curve" or line. Used to a great extent beginning in the eighteenth century, associated with Queen Anne–style furniture.

DAVENPORT. A small narrow desk with a writing slope above and drawers and cupboards below. The first desks of this type were made about 1790 to the order of a Captain Davenport, but most of the ones found now are mid-Victorian. The drawer fronts are often simulated, with a trick entrance to drawers on one side.

DENTIL. The under molding of a cornice, consisting of a series of small rectangular blocks or "teeth" set at equal distance from each other.

DESSERTE (French). A sideboard with an undershelf, and often with slide shelves on either side. Introduced in the Louis XVI period.

DOVETAIL. A tenon broader at its end than at its base, or a joint formed of one or more tenons fitting tightly within corresponding mortises.

DUMBWAITER. Consists of a central shaft carrying revolving circular trays, which terminated in a tripod base. Introduced about 1725, it remained popular during the Regency period. About 1820, quadruple supports replaced the earlier tripod variety.

DUST BOARD. A board placed between drawers, completely separating them. Not usually found on American case furniture.

EBONIZE. To treat wood by means of staining and polishing to resemble ebony.

ÉGLOMISÉ. Painting on glass, done on the reverse, frequently with gold leaf.

ENCOIGNURE (French). A corner cupboard of one or two parts. The top sometimes held a tier of shelves, but usually only the base has survived and has been covered with a marble top of a later date.

ESCRITOIRE (French). A writing desk or bureau.

ESCUTCHEON. A keyhole ornament, usually metal or ivory. Also a shield with armorial bearings or other devices.

ÉTAGÈRE (French). A tier of shelves for display of small objects. Referred to in Victorian times as a side 1 "whatnot."

FIDDLE-BACK. Used to describe a chair splat resembling a fiddle. In the Queen Anne period it appeared as the urn or vase-shaped splat, and again in the Empire period, as a shortened splat. It also describes the figuring of some veneers that resemble those usually found on the backs of old violins.

FINIAL. A decorative or ornamental termination at the top of a piece of furniture.

FLEMISH FOOT. A scroll foot formed by two intersecting and oppositely curved C scrolls.

FLUTING. A form of decoration in which channels or grooves run parallel to each other on a column or chair leg. A very popular motif in the Louis XVI period, and in the designs of Robert Adam and Thomas Sheraton. Derived from ancient classic forms, which were originally in marble.

FRET. An interlaced angular ornamental design sometimes applied on a solid background and sometimes reticulated.

FRIEZE. A plain or ornamental member under the crown or top of a piece of furniture or an entablature.

GADROON. A carved ornamental edging of repetitive forms, concave or convex, upright or twisted.

GATE-LEG TABLE. The descriptive name comes from the gate-like form of the two swing legs that support the raised leaves. It came into vogue in England in the mid-seventeenth century. Americans began making it about 1690. Size ranges from small occasional tables to very large ones, which can seat twelve to fourteen people. Small ones usually have a circular top, larger ones either oval or oblong. The central, fixed leaf is rectangular and relatively narrow. It is attached to the under structure of turned legs and stretchers. The under structure consists of four stationary and two swinging legs. Made by American cabinetmakers from 1690 to about 1750.

GESSO. A composition of size and plaster, molded in low relief and gilded. Applied to pieces of furniture, particularly side tables, mirror frames, and chairs. About 1690–1725.

GIRANDOLE. A candleholder of several branches often attached to a mirror frame to produce a brilliant lighting effect.

GUÉRIDON (French). A small round table or stand customarily used to hold a candelabrum.

GUILLOCHE (French). A form of ornament used for borders, friezes, and the like, consisting of a series of interlaced circles or ovals.

HIGHBOY. An American term for the English tallboy. First introduced in the latter part of the seventeenth century by the English, but elaborated and continued in use by American cabinetmakers. No longer being made after Chippendale's influence.

HITCHCOCK CHAIR (American). A fancy, painted, Sheraton-style chair manufactured in Connecticut by Lambert Hitchcock 1795–1852. Usually painted black and stenciled with floral patterns in gold. Some specimens have Hitchcock's name stenciled on the back edge of the seat. Hitchcock employed more than a hundred workers in his factory (1820–1850) at the height of his career. Again being produced.

HOOP BACK. A chair back in which the uprights and toprail continue in an unbroken line of curves.

HUTCH TABLE. A seventeenth-century armchair or settee, the back of which is a tabletop hinged on arms that can be lowered to form a table.

INLAY. A kind of ornament in which a recess is cut into the surface to be decorated and then filled with such materials as woods of different colors, ivory, mother-of-pearl, or metal.

KNEE. The upper, convex curve of a cabriole leg.

KNIFE BOX. A box, either urn-shaped or with a sloping top and serpentine front, having an interior filled with small slots into which knives and forks can be inserted for storage. They were made in pairs to be placed on either end of the side table. Introduced about 1760 and continued on in use.

LACQUERING. The process of applying many layers of paint and a special varnish that takes a very hard polish; also referred to as japanning.

LADDERBACK CHAIR. A chair with a back having horizontal slats between the uprights suggestive of a ladder. Originally these chairs had rush or split-oak seats. Chippendale designed mahogany chairs with transverse slats of carved and pierced mahogany.

LANCET ARCH. An arch that has an acutely pointed head.

LOWBOY (American). A low chest of several drawers on cabriole legs, usually made to match a highboy. Eighteenth century.

MARLBOROUGH LEG (also formerly spelled "Malbrow" and "Marlboro"). A trade term used by cabinetmakers in the eighteenth century for a leg of square section often ending in a block or similar foot. Chippendale adapted the square leg from the Chinese and mixed decorative motifs, using classic or Gothic to relieve the plainness of the simple form. In America, especially Philadelphia, the Marlborough leg gained popularity over the cabriole with claw-and-ball foot.

MARQUETRY. Veneered woodwork inlaid in very elaborate designs of varicolored woods.

MARTHA WASHINGTON CHAIR. A chair with a high stuffed back and open wooden arms, of the late eighteenth and early nineteenth centuries.

MÉRIDIENNE (French). A type of short sofa on which one can recline in a half-sitting position, but cannot lie down full length. Usually with one end much higher than the other. From the "meridian," "midday," or rest hour.

MONOPODIUM (French). A support for tables or other articles, in the shape of animals (lions or chimeras) having the head and body formed with a single leg and foot.

NÉCESSAIRE (French). A small case containing writing equipment or toilet accessories.

OGEE. A form made by two opposite cyma or wave curves with their convex sides meeting in a point.

OGEE FOOT. A swelled bracket foot, in the shape of a double curve, concave below and convex above.

ORMOLU. A term used for gilded bronze or a substitute of an alloy similar to brass to give the appearance of gold for furniture mounts.

OTTOMAN. A low stuffed seat without back. A stuffed—usually overstuffed—footstool.

PAD FOOT. A foot resembling the club foot but set on a disk.

PALMETTE. A conventionalized shape in the form of palmate leaves or sections, used as ornamentation.

PATERA. A small ornament—oval, round, or square—used as a base for decorative detail.

PAW FOOT. A terminal to the cabriole leg carved in the form of a lion's paw; mid-eighteenth century.

PEDIMENT. A member surmounting the cornice of bookcases, cupboards, cabinets, and so on. The unbroken form was popular from 1675 to 1760, the broken 1715 to 1800.

PEMBROKE TABLE. An occasional (or breakfast) table, perhaps so called because it was first ordered by the Countess of Pembroke. It is small, with two hinged flaps for extension on either side.

PIECRUST DECORATION. A raised edging, commonly employed in the decoration of mahogany tea and china tables during the third quarter of the eighteenth century. Scalloped, and resembling the outer edge of a piecrust.

PIER GLASS. A wall mirror hanging between windows, usually above a semicircular slab or pier table.

PILLAR AND CLAW. A term applied to circular tables of the eighteenth and early nineteenth centuries, made with a center pillar (or column) and claw feet.

PRESS. A cupboard or wardrobe used for storing linen.

QUARTERING. A method of ornamenting comparatively large surfaces, such as fall fronts to desks, with sheets of veneer. Two of the sheets from a set of four were sliced successively and had the same figure. They were reversed and placed side by side with the other two.

QUATREFOIL. A conventional adaptation of the four-leafed clover.

RECAMIER. A backless day bed of the Directoire and Empire periods having raised ends of equal height.

REEDING. The reverse of fluting; convex raised ornamentation in the form of a series of pipes or reeds, frequently found on chair and table legs at the end of the eighteenth century.

RÉGENCE (French). The period between 1715 and 1723, after the death of Louis XIV, and before Louis XV was of age, during which France was governed by the Duke of Orléans. Not to be confused with the English Regency, which is of much later date.

RIBBON BACK. Used to describe the ribbons of carved wood tied in bows that decorated the splats of chairs designed by Chippendale and illustrated in the *Director*. They are among the most sought after of all Chippendale designs.

ROMAYNE WORK. Ornamentation motif. Consists of roundels carved in low relief with human heads.

ROSETTES. Raised circular ornaments with flower decoration.

ROUNDEL. A circular background for ornamentation.

SABER LEG. A leg in the shape of a cavalry saber found on chairs of the Empire and Regency periods.

SALTIRE. An arrangement of stretchers in X form.

SCALLOP. A carved ornament resembling the scallop shell.

SCIMITAR FOOT. Any short leg or foot, such as for a pedestal table, having the form of an arc tangential to the floor. The name is suggested from the curved, simple-edged sword.

SCRIBE MARK. A mark on wood or metal made by a tool called a "scriber," to denote where the piece is to be cut or shaped.

SCROLL. An ornament of convolute form.

SEMAINIER (French). A tall piece of furniture with seven drawers, to hold linens for each day of the week.

SERPENTINE FRONT. The front of a piece of furniture in which the lines are wavy or curved.

SIDEBOARD. Although the term was used for a kind of side table, the first sideboards with flanking cupboards appeared during the Adam period. Hepplewhite, Sheraton, and Shearer designed many sideboards in a light and elegant style, often with curving fronts.

SLATS. The horizontal rails in a chair back.

SOFA TABLE. A table about five feet long and two feet in width, with drop leaves at either end, a central drawer or drawers in the frieze, and dummy drawers on the opposite side. Pedestal supports terminate in three or four feet; or there are end supports, lyre form or double legs on a curved base. Introduced toward the end of the eighteenth century to stand either in front of the sofa or along the back, some of the best sofa tables belonged to the Regency period. They were also made in America until about 1840, the best in the Federal style.

SPADE FOOT. A four-sided foot tapering to a base that resembles a spade.

SPANDREL. The approximately triangular corner space between the outer curve of an arch and the rectangle formed by the moldings enclosing it.

SPANISH FOOT. An outward-curved, somewhat square foot with carved ridges resembling claws.

SPLAT. That part of the chair back which lies above the seat and between the uprights on either side. Splats were either solid or pierced and often ornamented with marquetry or carvings.

SPOON BACK. A chair back curved to fit the back of the sitter. Especially popular during the Queen Anne period.

STRETCHERS. Rails, often turned, curved, or decoratively carved, that are placed between the legs of chairs and tables to reinforce them.

SWAG. A carved festoon of drapery, leaves, or flowers.

SWAN NECK. A curved pediment on cabinets.

SWELL FRONT. A convex curved front to a piece of case furniture.

TAMBOUR. A flexible shutter composed of narrow strips of wood glued side by side on canvas backing; often used for roll-top desks and closures for commodes.

TERMS, OR TERMINAL FIGURES. Supports or pedestals shaped as figures with natural heads, busts, and feet, and with the legs and lower bodies formed as tapering columns.

TESTER. The upper part or canopy of a high post bed.

TORCHÈRE (French). A flat-topped stand of considerable height intended to hold a candelabrum.

VENEER. A thin slice of any fine wood, which is applied to plain unfinished wood furniture and polished to produce an elegant and brilliant effect.

VOLUTES. Spiral-shaped ornaments used in the capitals of Ionic columns, in chair backs, and so forth.

WHATNOT. A term first used in the Regency period for a small rectanguar stand with shelves, designed to stand against a wall and intended to display objects, books, and so on. In its Victorian form it came into general use about 1840, grew in height, and by the 1850s was often designed for a corner.

Bibliography

Blake, J. P., and A. E. Reveirs-Hopkins. *Old English Furniture for the Small Collector*. London: B. T. Batsford, 1930.
———. *The Period of Queen Anne*. London: William Heinemann, 1911.
Burton, E. Milby. *Charleston Furniture 1700–1825*. Charleston, S.C.: Charleston Museum, 1955.
Butler, Joseph T. *American Antiques 1800–1900*. New York: Odyssey Press, 1965.
Coker, William Chambers, and Henry Roland Totten. *Trees of the Southeastern States*. Chapel Hill: University of North Carolina Press, 1945.
Cornelius, Charles Over. *Furniture Masterpieces of Duncan Phyfe*. New York: Dover, 1970.
Crawley, W. *Is It Genuine?* New York: Hart Publishing Co., 1972.
Downs, Joseph. *American Furniture, Queen Anne and Chippendale Periods*. New York: Macmillan Co., 1952.
Eberlein, Harold Donaldson, and Abbot McClure. *The Practical Book of Period Furniture*. Philadelphia and London: J.B. Lippincott Co., 1914.
Edwards, Ralph, and L. G. G. Ramsey. *The Connoisseur's Complete Period Guides*. New York: Bonanza Books, 1968.
Fastredge, Ralph. *English Furniture Styles*. Harmondsworth, Middlesex, England: Penguin Books, 1955.
Fine Hardwoods Association. *A World of Fine Hardwoods*. Chicago.
Gloag, John. *English Furniture*. London: Adam and Charles Black, 1952.

Hayden, Arthur, and Charles Messer Stow. *The Furniture Designs of Chippendale, Hepplewhite and Sheraton*. New York: Robert M. McBride & Co., 1938.

Heal, Ambrose. *London Furniture Makers 1660–1840*. London: B. T. Batsford, 1953.

Hinckley, F. Lewis. *Directory of the Historic Cabinet Woods*. New York: Crown Publishers, 1960.

Kinney, Ralph Parsons. *The Complete Book of Furniture Repair and Refinishing*. London and New York: Charles Scribner's Sons, 1950.

Lamb, George N. *The Mahogany Book*, 7th ed. Chicago: Mahogany Association, 1948.

Lees-Milne, James. *The Age of Adam*. London: B. T. Batsford, 1947.

Mallis, Arnold. *Handbook of Pest Control*, 3rd ed. New York: MacNair-Dorland Co., 1960.

Marsh, Moreton. *The Easy Expert in Collecting and Restoring American Antiques*. Philadelphia and New York: J.B. Lippincott Co., 1959.

Metropolitan Museum of Art. *19th Century America, Furniture and Other Decorative Arts*. Distributed by New York Graphic Society, 1970.

Miller, Edgar G., Jr. *American Antique Furniture, a Book for Amateurs*. New York: M. Barrows & Co., 1937.

Montgomery, Charles F. *American Furniture, the Federal Period 1788–1825*. New York: Viking Press, 1966.

Musgrave, Clifford. *Regency Furniture*. New York: Thomas Yoseloff, 1961.

Nutting, Wallace. *Furniture Treasury*. New York: Macmillan Co., 1948.

Ormsbee, Thomas H. *Care and Repair of Antiques*. New York: Gramercy Publishing Co., 1951.

———. *Field Guide to Early American Furniture*. New York: Bantam Books, 1961.

———. *The Story of American Furniture*. New York: Macmillan Co., 1937.

Reade, Brian. *Regency Antiques*. London: B. T. Batsford, 1953.

Singleton, Esther. *The Collecting of Antiques*. New York: Macmillan Co., 1937.

Teall, Gardner. *The Pleasures of Collecting*. New York: Century Co., 1920.

Ward-Jackson, Peter. *English Furniture Designs of the Eighteenth Century*. London: Her Majesty's Stationery Office, 1958.

Yates, Raymond F. *Antique Fakes and Their Detection*. New York: Gramercy Publishing Co., 1950.

Index

A NOTE ON THE TYPE

The text of this book was set in Electra, a Linotype face designed by W. A. Dwiggins (1880–1956), who was responsible for so much that is good in contemporary book design. Although much of his early work was in advertising and he was the author of the standard volume Layout in Advertising, *Mr. Dwiggins later devoted his prolific talents to book typography and type design and worked with great distinction in both fields. In addition to his designs for Electra, he created the Metro, Caledonia, and Eldorado series of type faces, as well as a number of experimental cuttings that have never been issued commercially.*

Electra cannot be classified as either modern or old-style. It is not based on any historical model, nor does it echo a particular period or style. It avoids the extreme contrast between thick and thin elements that marks most modern faces and attempts to give a feeling of fluidity, power, and speed.

COMPOSED BY MARYLAND LINOTYPE COMPOSITION CO., INC.,
BALTIMORE, MARYLAND

PRINTED BY MURRAY PRINTING,
FORGE VILLAGE, MASSACHUSETTS

BOUND BY THE BOOK PRESS,
BRATTLEBORO, VERMONT

COLOR LITHOGRAPHY BY
CREATIVE LITHOGRAPHERS,
NEW YORK